A Novel Pulpit

Sermons from George MacDonald's Fiction

Edited by
David L. Neuhouser

A Novel Pulpit
Copyright © 2010 David L. Neuhouser

WINGED LION PRESS
HAMDEN, CONNECTICUT

Winged Lion Press titles may be purchased for business or promotional use or special sales.

10-9-8-7-6-5-4-3-2-1

WINGED LION PRESS

ISBN   1-936294-03-6
ISBN 13   978-1-9362940-3-9

C. S. Lewis & Friends Book Series

With the cooperation of Winged Lion Press, the Center for the Study of C. S. Lewis & Friends at Taylor University plans to publish one volume of distinguished scholarship every two years. Our interest centers on work concerning C. S. Lewis, George MacDonald, Dorothy L. Sayers, Owen Barfield, and Charles Williams. Authors with book-length manuscripts who would like their work considered for future volumes may send a cover letter and proposal to Thom Satterlee, Program Director / Center for the Study of C. S. Lewis & Friends / Taylor University / Upland, IN 46989.

CONTENTS

Acknowledgments

A few years ago, a friend and colleague, Roger Phillips, expressed to me his appreciation of the sermons in *Annals of a Quiet Neighbourhood*, by George MacDonald. This comment led to the present book. Roger also read the first draft and made excellent suggestions that resulted in improvements. Also, thanks are due to Elaine Cooper who proofread the manuscript and whose comments and corrections improved the final result. Many others have encouraged, enlightened, and aided me in various ways. Among them are Barbara Amell, Leland Boren, Dan Bowell, Ed Brown, Ed Dinse, Frances White Ewbank, Dan and Elizabeth Hamilton, Rick Hill, Pamela Jordan-Long, Bill Ringenberg, Thom Satterlee, Daryl Yost, and most of all, my wife Ruth and our four children. Ruth is the first and most appreciated reader of my writing and sometimes the most appreciative. My apologies go to all others that I have omitted from this list due to my aging memory.

I am grateful to Taylor University for the opportunity to teach courses on MacDonald and related authors over the past two decades. Conversations with students in those classes have been an encouragement as well as a source of new insights. Papers and conversations at various conferences have been appreciated, especially at the C. S. Lewis and the Inklings Conferences and the Frances White Ewbank Colloquia on C. S. Lewis and Friends. An important research tool is the CD of MacDonald's complete works that Robert Trexler (Robert@WingedLionPress.com) has made available. The ability to search for words or phrases on the CD has been invaluable.

The Edwin W. Brown Collection in the Center for the Study of C. S. Lewis and Friends at Taylor University has been a valuable resource both for the materials in it and for the opportunities it has provided for interaction with MacDonald scholars from around the world, from Japan to Scotland and England. All of the members of the Lewis and Friends Committee have been helpful in many ways. Also, I am thankful for permission from Taylor University to include copies of photographs from the Edwin W. Brown Collection.

David L. Neuhouser
Scholar in Residence
Center for the Study of C. S. Lewis & Friends
Taylor University
Upland, Indiana

FOREWORD

George MacDonald was a popular author, preacher and lecturer in nineteenth-century England and Scotland. His American lecture tour in 1872 was a great success, culminating in a lucrative offer to become the pastor of a large New York City church. MacDonald wrote thirty novels, several volumes each of poetry, literary criticism, and sermons as well as numerous volumes of fairy tales and fantasy. "[T]hroughout the final third of the nineteenth century, George MacDonald's works were best sellers, and his status as a sage was secure. His novels sold, both in Great Britain and in the United States, by the hundreds of thousands of copies; his lectures were popular and widely attended; his poetry earned him at least passing consideration for the laureateship; and his reputation as a Christian teacher was vast." [Reis, p. 17] According to John Ruskin, MacDonald's book of devotional poetry, *Diary of an Old Soul*, "is one of the three great sacred poems of the nineteenth century." [Hein, p. 318] His poetry and collections of sermons have been helpful to generations of readers. His novels have exciting plots, colorful characters, and most of all, inspired Christian teaching. A comment by one critic, Michael Patrick Hearn, is typical of many literary critics' evaluation of his fairy tales: "Unquestionably, the master of the Victorian fairy tale was George MacDonald. His stories . . . were moral yet more symbolic than didactic or allegorical, as were many of his contemporaries' efforts." [Hearn, pp. xxiv-xxv]

G. K. Chesterton, W. H. Auden, C. S. Lewis, Madeleine L'Engle, Maurice Sendak, and Frederich Buechner are just some of the authors who have testified to the influence of MacDonald on their lives and works. C. S. Lewis said of George MacDonald, "I know hardly any other writer who seems to be closer, or more continually close, to the Spirit of Christ Himself." [Lewis, p. xxxv] Lewis also said, "I regarded him as my master, indeed I fancy that I never wrote a book that I did not quote from him." [Lewis, p. xxvii] Chesterton said that one fairy tale by MacDonald was the most realistic story he had ever read. Auden said, "In his power to project his inner life into images, events, beings, landscapes which are valid for all, he is one of the most remarkable writers of the nineteenth century." [George MacDonald, *The Visionary Novels*, p. vi] Madeleine L'Engle said, "Surely, George MacDonald is the grandfather of us all – all of us who struggle to come to terms with truth through fantasy." [MacDonald, *The Light Princess and other Fantasy Stories*, back cover page]

Another statement by L'Engle is one of the finest, certainly the most unusual and interesting, tributes to MacDonald. "My image of the Father, if I have to have one, is maternal, is, in fact, George MacDonald, so, yes, there is a beard, but there is also deep maternal love. It does not bother me that maternal is a feminine word, and George MacDonald was a male. When I call out to God in trouble or joy, as I often do, I think I am calling out to the whole Trinity, which is as far beyond our sexisms as love is beyond pornography." [L'Engle, pp. 221-222] I think MacDonald would like this. A curate in a MacDonald novel refers to God as "Father and Mother both in one." [MacDonald, *Adela Cathcart*, p. 184] In another of his novels, the hero receives this advice from his father: "And no man can be right manly … except he remember him who is father and mother both to all men." [MacDonald, *Castle Warlock*, p. 18]

There is increasing scholarly interest in MacDonald's work. There are four full-length biographies and several shorter ones, many books of literary criticism, and more than forty PhD dissertations. All of his books are now in print again. Another indication of his increasing popularity is shown by conferences featuring him. For example, in the five Frances White Ewbank Colloquia on C. S. Lewis and Friends held at Taylor University in Indiana since 1997, there have been many more papers on MacDonald than anyone else except Lewis himself. There have been at least three conferences in recent years on just MacDonald – the 2002 George MacDonald Summer School in Huntly, Scotland, the George MacDonald Centenary Conference at the University of Worcester in 2005 and the 2005 MacDonald Centenary Conference at Baylor University in Texas. There is a George MacDonald Society in Britain that publishes two periodicals, *North Wind* and *Orts*. In America, Barbara Amell edits a MacDonald quarterly, *Wingfold*. Interest in MacDonald is not confined to Britain and North America. Countries from around the world have been represented at the MacDonald conferences and in the published literature. For example, a book published in 2007, *George MacDonald's Challenging Theology of the Atonement, Suffering, and Death*, was written by the Japanese scholar, Miho Yamaguchi.

George MacDonald was born in 1824 in Huntly, Scotland. He received the Master of Arts degree from King's College, Aberdeen in 1845, having majored in the physical sciences. After a period as a tutor, he entered Highbury Seminary in London, a Congregational institution. In 1850, he accepted a pastorate at the Congregational Church in Arundel, a city south of London. His method of preaching was to write out the sermons, memorize them and then deliver them without notes. After only a few months in Arundel, he suffered hemorrhaging from the lungs and was confined to his bed for two months. This tuberculosis was to plague him from time to time throughout his life. Upon resuming his preaching duties in January of 1851, he had to curtail the length of his sermons. In a letter to his brother dated January 17, 1851, he wrote, "I will preach very briefly. Twenty minutes or so – and never mean to exceed half an hour after this." [Raeper, p. 82] Fifteen years later when writing *Annals of a Quiet Neighbourhood*, he still believed that a short sermon was best. In this novel Rev. Walton is preaching in an afternoon service and informs the reader,

The people had dined, and the usual somnolence followed. So I curtailed my sermon as much as I could omitting page after page of my manuscript; and when I came to a close, was rewarded by perceiving an agreeable surprise upon many of the faces round me. [Raeper, p. 85]

However, he did not hold to his resolution to preach for not more than thirty minutes and when he became a popular preacher in later years, his sermons were more than an hour in length.

George married Louisa Powell on March 8, 1851. In January of 1852, the first of their eleven children was born. However, after only two years in his pastorate at Arundel, there was dissatisfaction on the part of some of the leaders of the church with MacDonald's preaching and his salary was cut with the hope that this would force him to resign. However, upon receiving encouragement from some of the members, he persevered at the lower salary. It is not entirely clear what they were dissatisfied with. He was accused of being tainted with German theology although the accusers probably had only a dim understanding of what that was. More likely, the problem was MacDonald's insistence on obedience and particularly the duty of the rich to help the poor. It soon became apparent that it would cause a serious split in the church if he stayed, so he resigned.

He never held another pastorate. He did accept another one, but before he could begin he suffered another severe bout of tuberculosis. In fact, he never had a regular full-time job again. But he did not give up on his call to preach. In a letter to a friend on June 24, 1853, he wrote, "[P]reaching is my work, and preach I will somehow or other." [Raeper, p. 99]

MacDonald was forced to try many part-time jobs and various kinds of writing in order to support his family. He taught part time in colleges and lectured to various groups. He attempted to make a living as a poet, but was unable to support his growing family. Lady Byron, Lord Byron's widow, was impressed by his poetry and helped him with monetary gifts and arranged lectures for him. In general, fairy tales did not bring in much money and MacDonald's were no exception. Eventually, an editor advised him to write novels, which paid much better. However, he was constantly in need due to his large family, including foster children, poor health, and giving to those needier than himself. To bring in more money, his wife even adapted fairy tales and *Pilgrims Progress* as plays for her family to perform. Through all of this, MacDonald held fast to his dedication to preach the gospel of Jesus Christ.

In later life, MacDonald became a popular lecturer on literature and a popular guest preacher in a wide range of denominations. A person who heard him preach during his American tour recorded, as reprinted in the *Boston Daily Advertiser*,

> Last evening I went ... to hear George MacDonald preach ...
> He preached for a full hour, I should think. And I desire to
> record the profound impression which he made upon us all ... I
> never heard anything like it. He spoke without notes and with
> all the effect of extempore speech. There was no text. Nobody
> ever had such a manner, it was all his own, unique, not to be
> imitated, and yet so earnest, so free from any sign of effort or
> pretence, that it carried him straight to the best and inmost
> part of us. It was as if a father were pleading with his children,
> – his own feeling had melted away all that could obstruct the
> directness of his communication with us. The secret of it all
> was the simplicity and intensity of his feeling: he had become
> the very mouthpiece of the Divine Spirit, and we all heard
> and answered to him in our deepest hearts. This, indeed is
> preaching. [qtd. in Amell, p. 99]

MacDonald published five volumes of sermons during his lifetime
– *The Hope of the Gospel*, *The Miracles of Our Lord*, and *Unspoken
Sermons, Series I, II, and III*. These are all in print and available from
Johannessen Printing and Publishing. In addition to this, he also
published *God's Word to His Children*, a compilation of sermons. It has
been reprinted in paperback form by Regent College Publishing. The
sermons in *God's Word to His Children* were taken from the previous
collections, from periodicals, and from some of his novels – two from
Annals of a Quiet Neighbourhood and two from *The Seaboard Parish*.
These four sermons from his novels are the only ones that I am aware of
that have been previously published. In 1999, J. Flynn and D. Edwards
published *George MacDonald In The Pulpit*, a collection of MacDonald
sermons that had been published in Victorian periodicals. In her book
A Perfect Soul: George MacDonald in North America, Barbara Amell has
many contemporary newspaper accounts of the lectures and sermons
delivered during his tour of America. Amell also edits a MacDonald
periodical, *Wingfold*, in which she gives contemporary accounts of
some of his sermons. The Summer 2009 issue includes an article on
MacDonald reprinted from the *Christian World*, in which the writer
expresses the wish that MacDonald would preach more often. "Why
should he [MacDonald] not have gone on teaching from the pulpit

when he took to literature as the medium for fulfilling his vocation? Why not employ both vehicles? Is not such teaching as his especially needed now?" Actually, he did go on preaching both from the pulpit and in his novels, and his teaching is still relevant today.

MacDonald used his books and lectures to preach the gospel as much as he used his sermons. A correspondent to the *New York Post* in February of 1873 wrote, "George MacDonald's lecture on *Macbeth* is nothing more or less than a powerful sermon of sin and its consequences, with Shakespeare's tragedy as a text ... Dr. MacDonald is essentially a preacher: he preaches everywhere – in his poems and novels as well as in his sermons. And so in this lecture he lays hold of the great moral features of the play, which he considers and dwells upon, and impresses them in the true homiletic spirit." [qtd in Amell, p. 74] John Fraser, editor of the *American Athenaeum,* wrote an article for the *New York Independent* in which he said, "'Some people,' we once heard him [MacDonald] remark, 'accuse me of being too prone to turn my stories into sermons. They forget that I have another master than the public, and I must serve him first.'" [qtd. in Amell, p. 81]

MacDonald's novels are filled with Christian teaching. His son Ronald commented on this emphasis on preaching in his novels.

> Once I asked him why he did not, for a change and variety, write a story of mere human passion and artistic plot. He replied that he would like to write it. I asked him then further whether his highest literary quality was not in a measure injured by what must to many seem the monotony of his theme – referring to the novels alone. He admitted that this was possible; and went on to tell me that, that, having begun to do his work as a Congregational minister, and having been driven, by causes here inconvenient to be stated, into giving up that professional pulpit, he was no less impelled than compelled to use unceasingly the new platform whence he had found that his voice could carry so far. [Ronald MacDonald, pp. 32-33]

Ronald also gave the following as his father's purpose in writing novels. "[T]o carry once more the news which grows greater with age, to carry it with the freshness and new brilliance that come from the mouth of new poet to his own and succeeding generations, was none the less the moving principle of his life." [Ronald Macdonald, p.213]

In MacDonald's novels, the Christian teaching emerges out of the characters and story line, the narrator's comments, and inclusion of sermons given by the fictional preachers. These sermons in the novels are shorter than the ones in the collections of MacDonald's sermons and so are perhaps more accessible for some. In any case, they are both stimulating and thought provoking. It is my opinion that this collection of sermons from ten novels will bring the "freshness and brilliance" of MacDonald's message to a new generation. Each sermon has an introduction giving some explanation of the setting of the sermon or of the plot, if that is necessary for understanding the sermon. There may also be some conversations or remarks of the narrator in the quotation from the novel which have been included for better understanding.

Before going to the sermons themselves, I would like to share some of MacDonald's ideas about what preaching should and should not be. In *The Marquis of Lossie*, he wrote, "The custom of the time as to preaching was a sort of compromise between reading a sermon and speaking extempore, a mode morally as well as artistically false: the preacher learned his sermon by rote, and repeated it—as much like the man he therein was not, and as little like the parrot he was, as he could." [p. 102] In the same novel, he also describes a good preacher:

> At length the preacher rose to eloquence, an eloquence inspired by the hunger of his soul after truth eternal, and the love he bore to his brethren who fed on husks—an eloquence innocent of the tricks of elocution or the arts of rhetoric: to have discovered himself using one of them would have sent him home to his knees in shame and fear—an eloquence not devoid of discords, the strings of his instrument being now slack with emotion, now tense with vision, yet even in those discords shrouding the essence of all harmony. When he ceased, the silence that followed seemed instinct with thought, with that speech of the spirit which no longer needs the articulating voice. [pp. 145-146]

The following examples show what MacDonald thought preaching should not be. In *The Marquis of Lossie*, MacDonald told about a chapel where the object of the people was not to save its present congregation, but to gather a larger—ultimately that they might be saved, let us hope, but primarily that the drain upon the purses of those who were responsible for its rent and other outlays, might be lessened. Mr Masquar, therefore, to whom the post was a desirable one, had been mainly anxious that morning to prove his orthodoxy, and so commend his services. Not that in those days one heard so much of the dangers of heterodoxy: that monster was as yet but growling far off in the jungles of Germany; but certain whispers had been abroad concerning the preacher which he thought desirable to hush, especially as they were founded in truth. He had tested the power of heterodoxy to attract attention, but having found that the attention it did attract was not of a kind favourable to his wishes, had so skilfully remodelled his theories that, although to his former friends he declared them in substance unaltered, it was impossible any longer to distinguish them from the most uncompromising orthodoxy; and his sermon of that morning had tended neither to the love of God, the love of man nor a hungering after righteousness—its aim being to disprove the reported heterodoxy of Jacob Masquar. [pp. 105-106]In *Paul Faber, Surgeon*, he described a congregation thus:

For his people thought themselves intellectual, and certainly were critical. Mere edification was not enough for them. A large infusion of some polemic element was necessary to make the meat savory and such as their souls loved. Their ambition was not to grow in grace, but in social influence and regard – to glorify their dissent, not the communion of saints. Upon the chief corner-stone they would build their stubble of paltry religionism; they would set up their ragged tent in the midst of the eternal temple, their ragged tent in the midst of the eternal temple, careless how it blocked up the window and stair. [pp. 105-106]

In the same novel, he described a preacher:

… the flashy youth, proud of his small Latin and less Greek, a mere unit of the hundreds whom the devil of ambition drives to preaching; one who, whether the doctrines he taught were in the New Testament or not, certainly never found them there, being but the merest disciple of a disciple of a disciple, and fervid in words of which he perceived scarce a glimmer of the divine purport. [p. 46]

Also in Paul Faber, Surgeon is a description of how and why many chose to become ministers.

He had chosen preaching as a profession, just as so many take orders – with this difference from a large proportion of such, that he had striven powerfully to convince himself that he trusted in the merits of the Redeemer. Had he not in this met with tolerable success, he would not have yielded to the wish of his friends and left his father's shop in his native country-town for a dissenting college in the neighborhood of London. There he worked well, and became a good scholar, learning to read in the true sense of the word, that is, to try the spirits as he read. His character, so called, was sound, and his conscience, if not sensitive, was firm and regnant. But he was injured both spiritually and morally by some of the instructions there given. For one of the objects held up as duties before him, was to become capable of rendering himself acceptable to a congregation.

Most of the students were but too ready to regard, or at least to treat this object as the first and foremost of duties. The master-duty of devotion to Christ, and obedience to every word that proceeded out of His mouth, was very much treated as a thing understood, requiring little enforcement; while, the main thing demanded of them being sermons in some sense their own – honey culled at least by their own bees, and not bought in jars, much was said about the plan and composition of sermons, about style and elocution, and action – all plainly and confessedly, with a view to pulpit-success – the lowest of all low successes, and the most worldly. [p. 49]

Perhaps a good way to conclude these comments on preaching would be to give an example of a sermon from a fairy tale that MacDonald considered bad; that is, a fairy tale that gives false ideas about God and Christianity. This is similar to Lewis's method in *Screwtape Letters* in which he sheds light on Christianity by giving the devil's point of view. In the following examples, MacDonald gives a sermon and some comments that are contradictory to his own beliefs. In his fairy tale *The Princess and Curdie*, MacDonald described a church service in the wicked city of Gwyntystorm. The preacher was considered a very eloquent man, but I can offer only a few of the larger bones of his sermon. The main proof of the verity of their religion, he said, was that things always went well with those who profess it; and its first fundamental principle, grounded in inborn invariable instinct, was, that every One should take care of that One. This was the first duty of Man. If everyone would but obey this law, number one, then would everyone be perfectly cared for – one being always equal to one. But the faculty of care was in excess of need, and all that overflowed, and would otherwise run to waste, ought to be gently turned in the direction of one's neighbour, seeing that this also wrought for the fulfilling of the law, inasmuch as the reaction of excess so directed was upon the director of the same, to the comfort, that is, and well-being of the original self. To be just and friendly was to build the warmest and safest of all nests, and to be kind and loving was to line it with the softest of all furs and feathers, for the one precious, comfort-loving self there to lie, revelling in downiest bliss. [pp. 274-275]

In this satire, MacDonald is showing the incongruity of the "gospel of wealth" with the love of others that Jesus taught. This is just as relevant today as it was in the nineteenth century. The idea that a Christian preacher would be preaching such a self centered "gospel" is ludicrous. Although, we all would probably have to admit that the picture of living in a warm and safe nest with soft "furs and feathers" in "downiest bliss" is at times tempting to our "comfort-loving selves."

Finally, I attempted to find all of the sermons in MacDonald's novels. The novels of George MacDonald are divided into two classes, English and Scottish. The English are set in England while the Scottish ones are set in Scotland and contain Scottish dialect. There are a disproportionate number of sermons in the English novels as compared to the Scottish novels and more in his earlier books than in the later ones. I think that this is just due to the fact that to have a sermon in a novel there must be an important character who is a minister. For example, Thomas Wingfold preached sermons in three novels and Henry Walton, in two novels. Because MacDonald lived most of his adult life in England, he would be more familiar with English preachers and therefore would be more likely to appear in the English novels. The fact there are not as many sermons in the later novels does not mean that there is less Christian teaching in them. The comments on Christianity are in all of his novels but sometimes are given by the narrator or a character other than an ordained minister.

CHAPTER I

ANNALS OF A QUIET NEIGHBORHOOD

MacDonald's trilogy, *Annals of a Quiet Neighbourhood, The Seaboard Parish,* and *The Vicar's Daughter,* contains the story of a vicar in the town of Marshmallows - Henry Walton and his family. Marshmallows is generally thought to be a fictional version of Arundel where MacDonald had his only pastorate. Although many of MacDonald's portrayals of preachers are negative, Henry Walton is one of MacDonald's good characters and his sermons in the trilogy give MacDonald's beliefs. Following are sermons, preceded by excerpts from two chapters which give his ideas about preaching and set the stage, not only for the sermons in this chapter but for the rest of the book as well. Each section is headed by the chapter in *Annals of a Quiet Neighbourhood* from which the material is taken and the page numbers on which the sermon is found. Sometimes comments and some conversation other than the sermon are included to help understand the setting. It is interesting that "Sermon on God and Mammon" is given in this book and another version is given later by another preacher in *Paul Faber, Surgeon.*

"YOUNG WEIR"

I used now to wander about in the fields and woods, with a book in my hand, at which I often did not look the whole day, and which yet I liked to have with me. And I seemed somehow to come back with most upon those days in which I did not read. In this manner I prepared almost all my sermons that summer. But, although I prepared them thus in the open country, I had another custom, which perhaps may appear strange to some, before I preached them. This was, to spend the Saturday evening, not in my study, but in the church. This custom of mine was known to the sexton and his wife, and the church was always clean and ready for me after about mid-day, so that I could be alone there as soon as I pleased. It would take more space than my limits will afford to explain thoroughly why I liked to do this. But I will venture to attempt a partial explanation in a few words.

This fine old church in which I was honoured to lead the prayers of my people, was not the expression of the religious feeling of my time. There was a gloom about it—a sacred gloom, I know, and I loved it; but such gloom as was not in my feeling when I talked to my flock. I honoured the place; I rejoiced in its history; I delighted to think that even by the temples made with hands outlasting these bodies of ours, we were in a sense united to those who in them had before us lifted up holy hands without wrath or doubting; and with many more who, like us, had lifted up at least prayerful hands without hatred or despair. The place soothed me, tuned me to a solemn mood—one of self-denial, and gentle gladness in all sober things. But, had I been an architect, and had I had to build a church—I do not in the least know how I should have built it—I am certain it would have been very different from this. Else I should be a mere imitator, like all the church-architects I know anything about in the present day. For I always found the open air the most genial influence upon me for the production of religious feeling and thought. I had been led to try whether it might not be so with me by the fact that our Lord seemed so much to delight in the open air, and late in the day as well as early in the morning would climb the mountain to be alone with His Father. I found that it helped to give a reality to everything that I thought about, if I only contemplated it under the high untroubled blue, with the lowly green beneath my feet, and the wind blowing on me to remind me of the Spirit that once moved on the face of the waters, bringing order out of disorder and light out of darkness, and was now seeking every day a fuller entrance into my heart, that there He might work the one will of the Father in heaven.

My reader will see then that there was, as it were, not so much a discord, as a lack of harmony between the surroundings wherein my thoughts took form, or, to use a homelier phrase, my sermon was studied, and the surroundings wherein I had to put these forms into the garments of words, or preach that sermon. I therefore sought to bridge over this difference (if I understood music, I am sure I could find an expression exactly fitted to my meaning),—to find an easy passage between the open-air mood and the church mood, so as to be able to bring into the church as much of the fresh air, and the tree-music, and the colour-harmony, and the gladness over all, as might be possible; and, in order to this, I thought all my sermon over again in the afternoon sun as it shone slantingly through the stained window over Lord Eagleye's tomb, and in the failing light thereafter and the gathering dusk of the twilight, pacing up and down the solemn old place, hanging my thoughts here on a crocket, there on a corbel; now on the gable-point over which Weir's face would gaze next morning, and now on the aspiring peaks of the organ. I thus made the place a cell of thought and prayer. And when the next day came, I found the forms around me so interwoven with the forms of my thought, that I felt almost like one of the old monks who had built the place, so little did I find any check to my thought or utterance from its unfitness for the expression of my individual modernism. But not one atom the more did I incline to the evil fancy that God was more in the past than in the present; that He is more within the walls of the church, than in the unwalled sky and earth; or seek to turn backwards one step from a living Now to an entombed and consecrated Past [pp. 245-248]

"WHAT I PREACHED"

During the suffering which accompanied the disappointment at which I have already hinted, I did not think it inconsistent with the manly spirit in which I was resolved to endure it, to seek consolation from such a source as the New Testament—if mayhap consolation for such a trouble was to be found there. Whereupon, a little to my surprise, I discovered that I could not read the Epistles at all. For I did not then care an atom for the theological discussions in which I had been interested before, and for the sake of which I had read those epistles. Now that

I was in trouble, what to me was that philosophical theology staring me in the face from out the sacred page? Ah! reader, do not misunderstand me. All reading of the Book is not reading of the Word. And many that are first shall be last and the last first. I know NOW that it was Jesus Christ and not theology that filled the hearts of the men that wrote those epistles—Jesus Christ, the living, loving God-Man, whom I found—not in the Epistles, but in the Gospels. The Gospels contain what the apostles preached—the Epistles what they wrote after the preaching. And until we understand the Gospel, the good news of Jesus Christ our brother-king—until we understand Him, until we have His Spirit, promised so freely to them that ask it—all the Epistles, the words of men who were full of Him, and wrote out of that fulness, who loved Him so utterly that by that very love they were lifted into the air of pure reason and right, and would die for Him, and did die for Him, without two thoughts about it, in the very simplicity of NO CHOICE—the Letters, I say, of such men are to us a sealed book. Until we love the Lord so as to do what He tells us, we have no right to have an opinion about what one of those men meant; for all they wrote is about things beyond us. The simplest woman who tries not to judge her neighbour, or not to be anxious for the morrow, will better know what is best to know, than the best-read bishop without that one simple outgoing of his highest nature in the effort to do the will of Him who thus spoke.

But I have, as is too common with me, been led away by my feelings from the path to the object before me. What I wanted to say was this: that, although I could make nothing of the epistles, could see no possibility of consolation for my distress springing from them, I found it altogether different when I tried the Gospel once more. Indeed, it then took such a hold of me as it had never taken before. Only that is simply saying nothing. I found out that I had known nothing at all about it; that I had only a certain surface-knowledge, which tended rather to ignorance, because it fostered the delusion that I did know. Know that man, Christ Jesus! Ah! Lord, I would go through fire and water to sit the last at Thy table in Thy kingdom; but dare I say now I KNOW Thee!—But Thou art the Gospel, for Thou art the Way, the Truth, and the Life; and I have found

Thee the Gospel. For I found, as I read, that Thy very presence in my thoughts, not as the theologians show Thee, but as Thou showedst Thyself to them who report Thee to us, smoothed the troubled waters of my spirit, so that, even while the storm lasted, I was able to walk upon them to go to Thee. And when those waters became clear, I most rejoiced in their clearness because they mirrored Thy form—because Thou wert there to my vision—the one Ideal, the perfect man, the God perfected as king of men by working out His Godhood in the work of man; revealing that God and man are one; that to serve God, a man must be partaker of the Divine nature; that for a man's work to be done thoroughly, God must come and do it first Himself; that to help men, He must be what He is—man in God, God in man—visibly before their eyes, or to the hearing of their ears. So much I saw.

And therefore, when I was once more in a position to help my fellows, what could I want to give them but that which was the very bread and water of life to me—the Saviour himself? And how was I to do this?—By trying to represent the man in all the simplicity of His life, of His sayings and doings, of His refusals to say or do.—I took the story from the beginning, and told them about the Baby; trying to make the fathers and mothers, and all whose love for children supplied the lack of fatherhood and motherhood, feel that it was a real baby-boy. And I followed the life on and on, trying to show them how He felt, as far as one might dare to touch such sacred things, when He did so and so, or said so and so; and what His relation to His father and mother and brothers and sisters was, and to the different kinds of people who came about Him. And I tried to show them what His sayings meant, as far as I understood them myself, and where I could not understand them I just told them so, and said I hoped for more light by and by to enable me to understand them; telling them that that hope was a sharp goad to my resolution, driving me on to do my duty, because I knew that only as I did my duty would light go up in my heart, making me wise to understand the precious words of my Lord. And I told them that if they would try to do their duty, they would find more understanding from that than from any explanation I could give them ...

But it was not long either before my congregations began to improve, whatever might be the cause. I could not help hoping that it was really because they liked to hear the Gospel, that is, the good news about Christ himself. And I always made use of the knowledge I had of my individual hearers, to say what I thought would do them good. Not that I ever preached AT anybody; I only sought to explain the principles of things in which I knew action of some sort was demanded from them. For I remembered how our Lord's sermon against covetousness, with the parable of the rich man with the little barn, had for its occasion the request of a man that our Lord would interfere to make his brother share with him; which He declining to do, yet gave both brothers a lesson such as, if they wished to do what was right, would help them to see clearly what was the right thing to do in this and every such matter. Clear the mind's eye, by washing away the covetousness, and the whole nature would be full of light, and the right walk would speedily follow. [pp. 127-132]

"Sermon on God and Mammon"

This is a sermon that Walton preached on Christmas Day.

The Gospel according to St Matthew, the sixth chapter, and part of the twenty-fourth and twenty-fifth verses:—

"YE CANNOT SERVE GOD AND MAMMON. THEREFORE I SAY TO YOU, TAKE NO THOUGHT FOR YOUR LIFE.'

"When the Child whose birth we celebrate with glad hearts this day, grew up to be a man, He said this. Did He mean it?—He never said what He did not mean. Did He mean it wholly?—He meant it far beyond what the words could convey. He meant it altogether and entirely. When people do not understand what the Lord says, when it seems to them that His advice is impracticable, instead of searching deeper for a meaning which will be evidently true and wise, they comfort themselves by thinking He could not have meant it altogether, and so leave it. Or they think that if He did mean it, He could not expect them to carry it out. And in the fact that they could not do it perfectly if they were to try, they take refuge from the duty of trying to do it at all; or, oftener, they do not think about it at all as anything that in the least concerns them. The Son of our Father in heaven may have become a child, may have led the one life which belongs to every man to lead, may have suffered because we are sinners, may have died for our sakes, doing the will of His Father in heaven, and yet we have nothing to do with the words He spoke out of the midst of His true, perfect knowledge, feeling, and action! Is it not strange that it should be so? Let it not be so with us this day. Let us seek to find out what our Lord means, that we may do it; trying and failing and trying again—verily to be victorious at last—what matter WHEN, so long as we are trying, and so coming nearer to our end!

"MAMMON, you know, means RICHES. Now, riches are meant to be the slave—not even the servant of man, and not to be the master. If a man serve his own servant, or, in a word, any one who has no just claim to be his master, he is a slave. But here he serves his own slave. On the other hand, to serve God, the source of our being, our own glorious Father, is freedom; in fact, is the only way to get rid of all bondage. So you see plainly enough that a man cannot serve God and Mammon. For how can a slave of his own slave be the servant of the God of freedom, of Him who can have no one to serve Him but a free man? His service is freedom. Do not, I pray you, make any confusion between service and slavery. To serve is the highest, noblest calling in creation. For even the Son of man came not to be ministered unto, but to minister, yea, with Himself.

"But how can a man SERVE riches? Why, when he says to riches, "Ye are my good."

"When he feels he cannot be happy without them. When he puts forth the energies of his nature to get them. When he schemes and dreams and lies awake about them. When he will not give to his neighbour for fear of becoming poor himself. When he wants to have more, and to know he has more, than he can need. When he wants to leave money behind him, not for the sake of his children or relatives, but for the name of the wealth. When he leaves his money, not to those who NEED it, even of his relations, but to those who are rich like himself, making them yet more of slaves to the overgrown monster they worship for his size. When he honours those who have money because they have money, irrespective of their character; or when he honours in a rich man what he would not honour in a poor man. Then is he the slave of Mammon. Still more is he Mammon's slave when his devotion to his god makes him oppressive to those over whom his wealth gives him power; or when he becomes unjust in order to add to his stores.—How will it be with such a man when on a sudden he finds that the world has vanished, and he is alone with God? There lies the body in which he used to live, whose poor necessities first made money of value to him, but with which itself and its fictitious value are both left behind. He cannot now even try to bribe God with a cheque. The angels will not bow down to him because his property, as set forth in his will, takes five or six figures to express its amount. It makes no difference to them that he has lost it, though; for they never respected him. And the poor souls of Hades, who envied him the wealth they had lost before, rise up as one man to welcome him, not for love of him—no worshipper of Mammon loves another—but rejoicing in the mischief that has befallen him, and saying, "Art thou also become one of us? "And Lazarus in Abraham's bosom, however sorry he may be for him, however grateful he may feel to him for the broken victuals and the penny, cannot with one drop of the water of Paradise cool that man's parched tongue.

Alas, poor Dives! poor server of Mammon, whose vile god can pretend to deliver him no longer! Or rather, for the blockish god never pretended anything—it was the man's own doing—Alas for the Mammon-worshipper! he can no longer deceive himself in his riches. And so even in hell he is something nobler than he was on earth; for he worships his riches no longer. He cannot. He curses them.

Terrible things to say on Christmas Day! But if Christmas Day teaches us anything, it teaches us to worship God and not Mammon; to worship spirit and not matter; to worship love and not power.

Do I now hear any of my friends saying in their hearts: Let the rich take that! It does not apply to us. We are poor enough? Ah, my friends, I have known a light-hearted, liberal rich man lose his riches, and be liberal and light-hearted still. I knew a rich lady once, in giving a large gift of money to a poor man, say apologetically, "I hope it is no disgrace in me to be rich, as it is none in you to be poor." It is not the being rich that is wrong, but the serving of riches, instead of making them serve your neighbour and yourself—your neighbour for this life, yourself for the everlasting habitations. God knows it is hard for the rich man to enter into the kingdom of heaven; but the rich man does sometimes enter in; for God hath made it possible. And the greater the victory, when it is the rich man that overcometh the world. It is easier for the poor man to enter into the kingdom, yet many of the poor have failed to enter in, and the greater is the disgrace of their defeat. For the poor have more done for them, as far as outward things go, in the way of salvation than the rich, and have a beatitude all to themselves besides. For in the making of this world as a school of salvation, the poor, as the necessary majority, have been more regarded than the rich. Do not think, my poor friend, that God will let you off. He lets nobody off. You, too, must pay the uttermost farthing. He loves you too well to let you serve Mammon a whit more than your rich neighbour. Serve Mammon! do you say? 'How can I serve Mammon? I have no Mammon to serve.'—Would you like to have riches a moment sooner than God gives them? Would you serve Mammon if you had him?—'Who can tell?' do you answer? 'Leave those questions till I am tried.' But is there no bitterness in the tone of that response? Does it not mean, 'It will be a long time before I have a chance of trying THAT?'—But I am not driven to such questions for the chance of convicting some of you of Mammon-worship. Let us look to the text. Read it again.

"YE CANNOT SERVE GOD AND MAMMON. THEREFORE I SAY UNTO YOU, TAKE NO THOUGHT FOR YOUR LIFE."

"Why are you to take no thought? Because you cannot serve God and Mammon. Is taking thought, then, a serving of Mammon? Clearly.—Where are you now, poor man? Brooding over the frost? Will it harden the ground, so that the God of the sparrows cannot find food for His sons? Where are you now, poor woman? Sleepless over the empty cupboard and to-morrow's dinner? 'It is because we have no bread?' do you answer? Have you forgotten the five loaves among the five thousand, and the fragments that were left? Or do you know nothing of your Father in heaven, who clothes the lilies and feeds the birds? O ye of little faith? O ye poor-spirited Mammon-worshippers! who worship him not even because he has given you anything, but in the hope that he may some future day benignantly regard you. But I may be too hard upon you. I know well that our Father sees a great difference between the man who is anxious about his children's dinner, or even about his own, and the man who is only anxious to add another ten thousand to his much goods laid up for many years. But you ought to find it easy to trust in God for such a matter as your daily bread, whereas no man can by any possibility trust in God for ten thousand pounds. The former need is a God-ordained necessity; the latter desire a man-devised appetite at best—possibly swinish greed. Tell me, do you long to be rich? Then you worship Mammon. Tell me, do you think you would feel safer if you had money in the bank? Then you are Mammon-worshippers; for you would trust the barn of the rich man rather than the God who makes the corn to grow. Do you say—"What shall we eat? and what shall we drink? and wherewithal shall we be clothed?" Are ye thus of doubtful mind?—Then you are Mammon-worshippers. "But how is the work of the world to be done if we take no thought?—We are nowhere told not to take thought. We MUST take thought. The question is—What are we to take or not to take thought about? By some who do not know God, little work would be done if they were not driven by anxiety of some kind. But you, friends, are you content to go with the nations of the earth, or do you seek a better way—THE way that the Father of nations would have you walk in?

"WHAT then are we to take thought about? Why, about our work. What are we not to take thought about? Why, about our life. The one is our business: the other is God's. But you turn it the other way. You take no thought of earnestness about the doing of your duty; but you take thought of care lest God should not fulfill His part in the goings on of the world. A man's business is just to do his duty: God takes upon Himself the feeding and the clothing. Will the work of the world be neglected if a man thinks of his work, his duty, God's will to be done, instead of what he is to eat, what he is to drink, and wherewithal he is to be clothed? And remember all the needs of the world come back to these three. You will allow, I think, that the work of the world will be only so much the better done; that the very means of procuring the raiment or the food will be the more thoroughly used. What, then, is the only region on which the doubt can settle? Why, God. He alone remains to be doubted. Shall it be so with you? Shall the Son of man, the baby now born, and for ever with us, find no faith in you? Ah, my poor friend, who canst not trust in God—I was going to say you DESERVE—but what do I know of you to condemn and judge you?—I was going to say, you deserve to be treated like the child who frets and complains because his mother holds him on her knee and feeds him mouthful by mouthful with her own loving hand. I meant—you deserve to have your own way for a while; to be set down, and told to help yourself, and see what it will come to; to have your mother open the cupboard door for you, and leave you alone to your pleasures. Alas! poor child! When the sweets begin to pall, and the twilight begins to come duskily into the chamber, and you look about all at once and see no mother, how will your cupboard comfort you then? Ask it for a smile, for a stroke of the gentle hand, for a word of love. All the full-fed Mammon can give you is what your mother would have given you without the consequent loathing, with the light of her countenance upon it all, and the arm of her love around you.—And this is what God does sometimes, I think, with the Mammon-worshippers amongst the poor. He says to them, Take your Mammon, and see what he is worth. Ah, friends, the children of God can never be happy serving other than Him. The prodigal might fill his belly with riotous living or with the husks that the swine ate. It was all one, so long as he was not with his father. His soul was wretched. So would you be if you had wealth, for I fear you would only be worse Mammon-worshippers than now, and might well have to thank God for the misery of any swine-trough that could bring you to your senses.

"But we do see people die of starvation sometimes,—Yes. But

if you did your work in God's name, and left the rest to Him, that would not trouble you. You would say, If it be God's will that I should starve, I can starve as well as another. And your mind would be at ease. "Thou wilt keep him in perfect peace whose mind is stayed upon Thee, because he trusteth in Thee." Of that I am sure. It may be good for you to go hungry and bare-foot; but it must be utter death to have no faith in God. It is not, however, in God's way of things that the man who does his work shall not live by it. We do not know why here and there a man may be left to die of hunger, but I do believe that they who wait upon the Lord shall not lack any good. What it may be good to deprive a man of till he knows and acknowledges whence it comes, it may be still better to give him when he has learned that every good and every perfect gift is from above, and cometh down from the Father of lights.

"I SHOULD like to know a man who just minded his duty and troubled himself about nothing; who did his own work and did not interfere with God's. How nobly he would work—working not for reward, but because it was the will of God! How happily he would receive his food and clothing, receiving them as the gifts of God! What peace would be his! What a sober gaiety! How hearty and infectious his laughter! What a friend he would be! How sweet his sympathy! And his mind would be so clear he would understand everything. His eye being single, his whole body would be full of light. No fear of his ever doing a mean thing. He would die in a ditch, rather. It is this fear of want that makes men do mean things. They are afraid to part with their precious lord—Mammon. He gives no safety against such a fear. One of the richest men in England is haunted with the dread of the workhouse. This man whom I should like to know, would be sure that God would have him liberal, and he would be what God would have him. Riches are not in the least necessary to that. Witness our Lord's admiration of the poor widow with her great farthing.

"But I think I hear my troubled friend who does not love money, and yet cannot trust in God out and out, though she fain would,—I think I hear her say, "I believe I could trust Him for myself, or at least I should be ready to dare the worst for His sake; but my children —it is the thought of my children that is too much for me." Ah, woman! she whom the Saviour praised so pleasedly, was one who trusted Him for her daughter. What an honour she had! "Be it unto thee even as thou wilt." Do you think you love your children better than He who made them? Is not your love what it is because He put it into your heart first? Have not you often been cross with them? Sometimes unjust to them? Whence came the returning love that rose from unknown depths in your being, and swept away the anger and the injustice! You did not create that love. Probably you were not good enough to send for it by prayer. But it came. God sent it. He makes you love your children; be sorry when you have been cross with them; ashamed when you have been unjust to them; and yet you won't trust Him to give them food and clothes! Depend upon it, if He ever refuses to give them food and clothes, and you knew all about it, the why and the wherefore, you would not dare to give them food or clothes either. He loves them a thousand times better than you do—be sure of that—and feels for their sufferings too, when He cannot give them just what He would like to give them—cannot for their good, I mean.

"But as your mistrust will go further, I can go further to meet it. You will say, 'Ah! Yes'—in your feeling, I mean, not in words,—you will say, 'Ah! yes—food and clothing of a sort! Enough to keep life in and too much cold out! But I want my children to have plenty of GOOD food, and NICE clothes.'

"Faithless mother! Consider the birds of the air. They have so much that at least they can sing! Consider the lilies—they were red lilies, those. Would you not trust Him who delights in glorious colours—more at least than you, or He would never have created them and made us to delight in them? I do not say that your children shall be clothed in scarlet and fine linen; but if not, it is not because God despises scarlet and fine linen or does not love your children. He loves them, I say, too much to give them everything all at once. But He would make them such that they may have everything without being the worse, and with being the better for it. And if you cannot trust Him yet, it begins to be a shame, I think.

"It has been well said that no man ever sank under the burden of the day. It is when to-morrow's burden is added to the burden of to-day, that the weight is more than a man can bear. Never load yourselves so, my friends. If you find yourselves so loaded, at least remember this: it is your own doing, not God's. He begs you to leave the future to Him, and mind the present. What more or what else could He do to take the burden off you? Nothing else would do it. Money in the bank wouldn't do it. He cannot do to-morrow's business for you beforehand to save you from fear about it. That would derange everything. What else is there but to tell you to trust in Him, irrespective of the fact that nothing else but such trust can put our heart at peace, from the very nature of our relation to Him as well as the fact that we need these things. We think that we come nearer to God than the lower animals do by our foresight. But there is another side to it. We are like to Him with whom there is no past or future, with whom a day is as a thousand years, and a thousand years as one day, when we live with large bright spiritual eyes, doing our work in the great present, leaving both past and future to Him to whom they are ever present, and fearing nothing, because He is in our future, as much as He is in our past, as much as, and far more than, we can feel Him to be in our present. Partakers thus of the divine nature, resting in that perfect All-in-all in whom our nature is eternal too, we walk without fear, full of hope and courage and strength to do His will, waiting for the endless good which He is always giving as fast as He can get us able to take it in. Would not this be to be more of gods than Satan promised to Eve? To live carelessly-divine, duty-doing, fearless, loving, self-forgetting lives—is not that more than to know both good and evil—lives in which the good, like Aaron's rod, has swallowed up the evil, and turned it into good? For pain and hunger are evils: but if faith in God swallows them up, do they not so turn into good? I say they do. And I am glad to believe that I am not alone in my parish in this conviction. I have never been too hungry, but I have had trouble which I would gladly have exchanged for hunger and cold and weariness. Some of you have known hunger and cold and weariness. Do you not join with me to say: It is well, and better than well—whatever helps us to know the love of Him who is our God?

"But there HAS BEEN just one man who has acted thus. And

it is His Spirit in our hearts that makes us desire to know or to be another such—who would do the will of God for God, and let God do God's will for Him. For His will is all. And this man is the baby whose birth we celebrate this day. Was this a condition to choose—that of a baby—by one who thought it part of a man's high calling to take care of the morrow? Did He not thus cast the whole matter at once upon the hands and heart of His Father? Sufficient unto the baby's day is the need thereof; he toils not, neither does he spin, and yet he is fed and clothed, and loved, and rejoiced in. Do you remind me that sometimes even his mother forgets him—a mother, most likely, to whose self-indulgence or weakness the child owes his birth as hers? Ah! but he is not therefore forgotten, however like things it may look to our half-seeing eyes, by his Father in heaven. One of the highest benefits we can reap from understanding the way of God with ourselves is, that we become able thus to trust Him for others with whom we do not understand His ways.

"But let us look at what will be more easily shown—how, namely, He did the will of His Father, and took no thought for the morrow after He became a man. Remember how He forsook His trade when the time came for Him to preach. Preaching was not a profession then. There were no monasteries, or vicarages, or stipends, then. Yet witness for the Father the garment woven throughout; the ministering of women; the purse in common! Hard-working men and rich ladies were ready to help Him, and did help Him with all that He needed.—Did He then never want? Yes; once at least—for a little while only.

"He was a-hungered in the wilderness. Make bread,' said Satan. 'No,' said our Lord.—He could starve; but He could not eat bread that His Father did not give Him, even though He could make it Himself. He had come hither to be tried. But when the victory was secure, lo! the angels brought Him food from His Father.—Which was better? To feed Himself, or be fed by His Father? [Judge]? yourselves, [anxious] people, He sought the kingdom of God and His righteousness, and the bread was added unto Him.

"And this gives me occasion to remark that the same truth holds with regard to any portion of the future as well as the morrow. It is a principle, not a command, or an encouragement, or a promise merely. In respect of it there is no difference between next day and next year, next hour and next century. You will see at once the absurdity of taking no thought for the morrow, and taking thought for next year. But do you see likewise that it is equally reasonable to trust God for the next moment, and equally unreasonable not to trust Him? The Lord was hungry and needed food now, though He could still go without for a while. He left it to His Father. And so He told His disciples to do when they were called to answer before judges and rulers. 'Take no thought. It shall be given you what ye shall say.' You have a disagreeable duty to do at twelve o'clock. Do not blacken nine and ten and eleven, and all between, with the colour of twelve. Do the work of each, and reap your reward in peace. So when the dreaded moment in the future becomes the present, you shall meet it walking in the light, and that light will overcome its darkness. How often do men who have made up their minds what to say and do under certain expected circumstances, forget the words and reverse the actions! The best preparation is the present well seen to, the last duty done. For this will keep the eye so clear and the body so full of light that the right action will be perceived at once, the right words will rush from the heart to the lips, and the man, full of the Spirit of God because he cares for nothing but the will of God, will trample on the evil thing in love, and be sent, it may be, in a chariot of fire to the presence of his Father, or stand unmoved amid the cruel mockings of the men he loves.

"Do you feel inclined to say in your hearts: 'It was easy for Him to take no thought, for He had the matter in His own hands?' But observe, there is nothing very noble in a man's taking no thought except it be from faith. If there were no God to take thought for us, we should have no right to blame any one for taking thought. You may fancy the Lord had His own power to fall back upon. But that would have been to Him just the one dreadful thing. That His Father should forget Him!—no power in Himself could make up for that. He feared nothing for Himself; and never once employed His divine power to save Him from His human fate. Let God do that for Him if He saw fit. He did not come into the world to take care of Himself. That would not be in any way divine. To fall back on Himself,

God failing Him—how could that make it easy for Him to avoid care? The very idea would be torture. That would be to declare heaven void, and the world without a God. He would not even pray to His Father for what He knew He should have if He did ask it. He would just wait His will.

"But see how the fact of His own power adds tenfold significance to the fact that He trusted in God. We see that this power would not serve His need—His need not being to be fed and clothed, but to be one with the Father, to be fed by His hand, clothed by His care. This was what the Lord wanted—and we need, alas! too often without wanting it. He never once, I repeat, used His power for Himself. That was not his business. He did not care about it. His life was of no value to Him but as His Father cared for it. God would mind all that was necessary for Him, and He would mind the work His Father had given Him to do. And, my friends, this is just the one secret of a blessed life, the one thing every man comes into this world to learn. With what authority it comes to us from the lips of Him who knew all about it, and ever did as He said!

"Now you see that He took no thought for the morrow. And, in the name of the holy child Jesus, I call upon you, this Christmas day, to cast care to the winds, and trust in God; to receive the message of peace and good-will to men; to yield yourselves to the Spirit of God, that you may be taught what He wants you to know; to remember that the one gift promised without reserve to those who ask it—the one gift worth having—the gift which makes all other gifts a thousand-fold in value, is the gift of the Holy Spirit, the spirit of the child Jesus, who will take of the things of Jesus, and show them to you—make you understand them, that is—so that you shall see them to be true, and love Him with all your heart and soul, and your neighbour as yourselves." [pp. 192-208]

"THE DEVIL IN THE VICAR"

I lingered on long in the dark church, as my reader knows I had done often before. Nor did I move from the seat I had first taken till I left the sacred building. And there I made my sermon for the next morning. And herewith I impart it to my reader. But he need not be afraid of another such as I have already given him, for I impart it only in its original germ, its concentrated essence of sermon—these four verses:

> Had I the grace to win the grace
>   Of some old man complete in lore,
> My face would worship at his face,
>   Like childhood seated on the floor.
>
> Had I the grace to win the grace
>   Of childhood, loving shy, apart,
> The child should find a nearer place,
>   And teach me resting on my heart.
>
> Had I the grace to win the grace
>   Of maiden living all above,
> My soul would trample down the base,
>   That she might have a man to love.
>
> A grace I have no grace to win
>   Knocks now at my half-open door:
> Ah, Lord of glory, come thou in,
>   Thy grace divine is all and more.

This was what I made for myself. I told my people that God had created all our worships, reverences, tendernesses, loves. That they had come out of His heart, and He had made them in us because they were in Him first. That otherwise He would not have cared to make them. That all that we could imagine of the wise, the lovely, the beautiful, was in Him, only infinitely more of them than we could not merely imagine, but understand, even if He did all He could to explain them to us, to make us understand them. That in Him was all the wise teaching of the best man ever known in the world and more; all the grace and gentleness and truth of the best child and more; all the tenderness and devotion of the truest type of womankind and more; for there is a love that passeth the love of woman, not the love of Jonathan to David, though David said so: but the love of God to the men and women whom He has made. Therefore, we must be all God's; and all our aspirations, all our worships, all our honours, all our loves, must centre in Him, the Best. [pp. 422-424]

"A Sermon to Myself"

In this chapter, the sermon is not given exactly but Walton describes his sermon and his feelings and thoughts about it.

All at once the remembrance crossed my mind of a sermon I had preached before upon the words of St Paul: "Thou therefore which teachest another, teachest thou not thyself?" a subject suggested by the fact that on the preceding Sunday I had especially felt, in preaching to my people, that I was exhorting myself whose necessity was greater than theirs—at least I felt it to be greater than I could know theirs to be. And now the converse of the thought came to me, and I said to myself, "Might I not try the other way now, and preach to myself? In teaching myself, might I not teach others? Would it not hold? I am very troubled and faithless now. If I knew that God was going to lay the full weight of this grief upon me, yet if I loved Him with all my heart, should I not at least be more quiet? There would not be a storm within me then, as if the Father had descended from the throne of the heavens, and 'chaos were come again.' Let me expostulate with myself in my heart, and the words of my expostulation will not be the less true with my people."

All this passed through my mind as I sat in my study after breakfast, with the great old cedar roaring before my window. It was within an hour of church-time. I took my Bible, read and thought, got even some comfort already, and found myself in my vestry not quite unwilling to read the prayers and speak to my people.

There were very few present. The day was one of the worst—violently stormy, which harmonized somewhat with my feelings … Instead of finding myself a mere minister to the prayers of others, I found, as I read, that my heart went out in crying to God for the divine presence of His Spirit. And if I thought more of myself in my prayers than was well, yet as soon as I was converted, would I not strengthen my brethren? And the sermon I preached to myself and through myself to my people, was that which the stars had preached to me, and thereby driven me to my knees by the mill-door. I took for my text,

"The glory of the Lord shall be revealed;" and then I proceeded
to show them how the glory of the Lord was to be revealed. I
preached to myself that throughout this fortieth chapter of the
prophecies of Isaiah, the power of God is put side by side with
the weakness of men, not that He, the perfect, may glory over
His feeble children; not that He may say to them—"Look how
mighty I am, and go down upon your knees and worship"—for
power alone was never yet worthy of prayer; but that he may
say thus: "Look, my children, you will never be strong but with
MY strength. I have no other to give you. And that you can
get only by trusting in me. I cannot give it you any other way.
There is no other way. But can you not trust in me? Look how
strong I am. You wither like the grass. Do not fear. Let the
grass wither. Lay hold of my word, that which I say to you out
of my truth, and that will be life in you that the blowing of the
wind that withers cannot reach. I am coming with my strong
hand and my judging arm to do my work. And what is the
work of my strong hand and ruling arm? To feed my flock like
a shepherd, to gather the lambs with my arm, and carry them
in my bosom, and gently lead those that are with young. I have
measured the waters in the hollow of my hand, and held the
mountains in my scales, to give each his due weight, and all
the nations, so strong and fearful in your eyes, are as nothing
beside my strength and what I can do. Do not think of me as
of an image that your hands can make, a thing you can choose
to serve, and for which you can do things to win its favour. I
am before and above the earth, and over your life, and your
oppressors I will wither with my breath. I come to you with
help. I need no worship from you. But I say love me, for love is
life, and I love you. Look at the stars I have made. I know every
one of them. Not one goes wrong, because I keep him right.
Why sayest thou, O Jacob, and speakest, O Israel—my way is
HID from the Lord, and my judgment is passed over from my
God! I give POWER to the FAINT, and to them that have no
might, plenty of strength."

"Thus," I went on to say, "God brings His strength to destroy
our weakness by making us strong. This is a God indeed! Shall
we not trust Him?"

... And then I tried to show them that it was in the commonest troubles of life, as well as in the spiritual fears and perplexities that came upon them, that they were to trust in God; for God made the outside as well as the inside, and they altogether belonged to Him; and that when outside things, such as pain or loss of work, or difficulty in getting money, were referred to God and His will, they too straightway became spiritual affairs, for nothing in the world could any longer appear common or unclean to the man who saw God in everything. But I told them they must not be too anxious to be delivered from that which troubled them: but they ought to be anxious to have the presence of God with them to support them, and make them able in patience to possess their souls; and so the trouble would work its end—the purification of their minds, that the light and gladness of God and all His earth, which the pure in heart and the meek alone could inherit, might shine in upon them. And then I repeated to them this portion of a prayer out of one of Sir Philip Sidney's books:—

"O Lord, I yield unto Thy will, and joyfully embrace what sorrow Thou wilt have me suffer. Only thus much let me crave of Thee, (let my craving, O Lord, be accepted of Thee, since even that proceeds from Thee,) let me crave, even by the noblest title, which in my greatest affliction I may give myself, that I am Thy creature, and by Thy goodness (which is Thyself) that Thou wilt suffer some beam of Thy majesty so to shine into my mind, that it may still depend confidently on Thee."

All the time I was speaking, the rain, mingled with sleet, was dashing against the windows, and the wind was howling over the graves all about. But the dead were not troubled by the storm; and over my head, from beam to beam of the roof, now resting on one, now flitting to another, a sparrow kept flying, which had taken refuge in the church till the storm should cease and the sun shine out in the great temple. "This," I said aloud, "is what the church is for: as the sparrow finds there a house from the storm, so the human heart escapes thither to hear the still small voice of God when its faith is too weak to find Him in the storm, and in the sorrow, and in the pain." And while I spoke, a dim watery gleam fell on the chancel-floor, and the comfort of the sun awoke in my heart. Nor let any one call me superstitious for taking that pale sun-ray of hope as sent to me; for I received it as comfort for the race, and for me as one of the family, even as the bow that was set in the cloud, a promise to the eyes of light for them that sit in darkness. As I write, my eye falls upon the Bible on the table by my side, and I read the words, "For the Lord God is a sun and shield, the Lord will give grace and glory." And I lift my eyes from my paper and look abroad from my window, and the sun is shining in its strength. The leaves are dancing in the light wind that gives them each its share of the sun, and my trouble has passed away for ever, like the storm of that night and the unrest of that strange Sabbath.

Such comforts would come to us oftener from Nature, if we really believed that our God was the God of Nature; that when He made, or rather when He makes, He means; that not His hands only, but His heart too, is in the making of those things; that, therefore, the influences of Nature upon human minds and hearts are because He intended them. And if we believe that our God is everywhere, why should we not think Him present even in the coincidences that sometimes seem so strange? For, if He be in the things that coincide, He must be in the coincidence of those things.

Miss Oldcastle told me once that she could not take her eyes off a butterfly which was flitting about in the church all the time I was speaking of the resurrection of the dead. I told the people that in Greek there was one word for the soul and for a butterfly—Psyche; that I thought as the light on the rain made the natural symbol of mercy—the rainbow, so the butterfly was the type in nature, and made to the end, amongst other ends, of being such a type—of the resurrection of the human body; that its name certainly expressed the hope of the Greeks in immortality, while to us it speaks likewise of a glorified body, whereby we shall know and love each other with our eyes as well as our hearts.—My sister saw the butterfly too, but only remembered that she had seen it when it was mentioned in her hearing: on her the sight made no impression; she saw no coincidence.

I descended from the pulpit comforted by the sermon I had preached to myself. But I was glad to feel justified in telling my people that, in consequence of the continued storm, for there had been no more of sunshine than just that watery gleam, there would be no service in the afternoon, and that I would instead visit some of my sick poor, whom the weather might have discomposed in their worn dwellings. [pp. 511-517]

❖ Chapter 2 ❖

THE SEABOARD PARISH

This chapter continues Henry Walton's sermons, this time from the second book of the trilogy, *The Seaboard Parish.*

"MY FIRST SERMON IN THE SEABOARD PARISH"

There had been a shipwreck caused by a violent storm and the shipwrecked sailors were in the congregation for this sermon.

I gave them no text. I had one myself, which was the necessary thing. They should have it by and by.

"Once upon a time," I said, "a man went up a mountain, and stayed there till it was dark, and stayed on. Now, a man who finds himself on a mountain as the sun is going down, especially if he is alone, makes haste to get down before it is dark. But this man went up when the sun was going down, and, as I say, continued there for a good long while after it was dark. You will want to know why. I will tell you. He wished to be alone. He hadn't a house of his own. He never had all the time he lived. He hadn't even a room of his own into which he could go, and bolt the door of it. True, he had kind friends, who gave him a bed: but they were all poor people, and their houses were small, and very likely they had large families, and he could not always find a quiet place to go into. And I dare say, if he had had a room, he would have been a little troubled with the children constantly coming to find him; for however much he loved them—and no man was ever so fond of children as he was—he needed to be left quiet sometimes. So, upon this occasion, he went up the mountain just to be quiet. He had been all day with a crowd of people, and he felt that it was time to be alone. For he had been talking with men all day, which tires and sometimes confuses a man's thoughts, and now he wanted to talk with God—for that makes a man strong, and puts all the confusion in order again, and lets a man know what he is about. So he went to the top of the hill. That was his secret chamber. It had no door; but that did not matter—no one could see him but God. There he stayed for hours—sometimes, I suppose, kneeling in his prayer to God; sometimes sitting, tired with his own thinking, on a stone; sometimes walking about, looking forward to what would come next—not anxious about it, but contemplating it. For just before he came up here, some of the people who had been with him wanted to make him a king; and this would not do—this was not what God wanted of him, and therefore he got rid of them, and came up here to talk to God. It was so quiet up here! The earth had almost vanished. He could see just the bare hilltop beneath him, a glimmer below, and the sky and the stars over his head. The people had all gone away to their own homes, and perhaps next day would hardly think about him at all, busy catching fish, or digging their gardens, or making things for their houses. But he knew that God would not forget him the next day any more than this day, and that God had sent him not to be the king that these people wanted him to be, but their servant. So, to make his heart strong, I say, he went up into the mountain alone to have a talk with his Father. How quiet it all was up here, I say, and how noisy it had been down there a little while ago! But God had been in the noise then as much as he was in the quiet now—the only difference being that he could not then be alone with him. I need not tell you who this man was—it was the king of men, the servant of men, the Lord Jesus Christ, the everlasting son of our Father in heaven.

"Now this mountain on which he was praying had a small lake at the foot of it—that is, about thirteen miles long, and five miles broad. Not wanting even his usual companions to be with him this evening—partly, I presume, because they were of the same mind as those who desired to take him by force and make him a king—he had sent them away in their boat, to go across this water to the other side, where were their homes and their families. Now, it was not pitch dark either on the mountain-top or on the water down below; yet I doubt if any other man than he would have been keen-eyed enough to discover that little boat down in the middle of the lake, much distressed by the west wind that blew right in their teeth. But he loved every man in it so much, that I think even as he was talking to his Father, his eyes would now and then go looking for and finding it—watching it on its way across to the other side. You must remember that it was a little boat; and there are often tremendous storms upon these small lakes with great mountains about them. For the wind will come all at once, rushing down through the clefts in as sudden a squall as ever overtook a sailor at sea. And then, you know, there is no sea-room. If the wind get the better of them, they are on the shore in a few minutes, whichever way the wind may blow. He saw them worn out at the oar, toiling in rowing, for the wind was contrary unto them. So the time for loneliness and prayer was over, and the time to go down out of his secret chamber and help his brethren was come. He did not need to turn and say good-bye to his Father, as if he dwelt on that mountain-top alone: his Father was down there on the lake as well. He went straight down. Could not his Father, if he too was down on the lake, help them without him? Yes. But he wanted him to do it, that they might see that he did it. Otherwise they would only have thought that the wind fell and the waves lay down, without supposing for a moment that their Master or his Father had had anything to do with it. They would have done just as people do now-a-days: they think that the help comes of itself, instead of by the will of him who determined from the first that men should be helped. So the Master went down the hill. When he reached the border of the lake, the wind being from the other side, he must have found the waves breaking furiously upon the rocks. But that made no difference to him. He looked out as he stood alone on the edge amidst the rushing wind and the noise of the water, out over the waves under the clear, starry sky, saw where the tiny boat was tossed about like a nutshell, and set out."

The mariners had been staring at me up to this point, leaning forward on their benches, for sailors are nearly as fond of a good yarn as they are of tobacco; and I heard afterwards that they had voted parson's yarn a good one. Now, however, I saw one of them, probably more ignorant than the others, cast a questioning glance at his neighbour. It was not returned, and he fell again into a listening attitude. He had no idea of what was coming. He probably thought parson had forgotten to say how Jesus had come by a boat.

"The companions of our Lord had not been willing to go away and leave him behind. Now, I dare say, they wished more than ever that he had been with them—not that they thought he could do anything with a storm, only that somehow they would have been less afraid with his face to look at. They had seen him cure men of dreadful diseases; they had seen him turn water into wine—some of them; they had seen him feed five thousand people the day before with five loaves and two small fishes; but had one of their number suggested that if he had been with them, they would have been safe from the storm, they would not have talked any nonsense about the laws of nature, not having learned that kind of nonsense, but they would have said that was quite a different thing—altogether too much to expect or believe: *nobody* could make the wind mind what it was about, or keep the water from drowning you if you fell into it and couldn't swim; or such-like.

"At length, when they were nearly worn out, taking feebler and feebler strokes, sometimes missing the water altogether, at other times burying their oars in it up to the handles—as they rose on the crest of a huge wave, one of them gave a cry, and they all stopped rowing and stared, leaning forward to peer through the darkness. And through the spray which the wind tore from the tops of the waves and scattered before it like dust, they saw, perhaps a hundred yards or so from the boat, something standing up from the surface of the water. It seemed to move towards them. It was a shape like a man. They all cried out with fear, as was natural, for they thought it must be a ghost."

How the faces of the sailors strained towards me at this part of the story! I was afraid one of them especially was on the point of getting up to speak, as we have heard of sailors doing in church. I went on.

"But then, over the noise of the wind and the waters came the voice they knew so well. It said, 'Be of good cheer: it is I. Be not afraid.' I should think, between wonder and gladness, they hardly knew for some moments where they were or what they were about. Peter was the first to recover himself apparently. In the first flush of his delight he felt strong and full of courage. 'Lord, if it be thou,' he said, 'bid me come unto thee on the water.' Jesus just said, 'Come;' and Peter unshipped his oar, and scrambled over the gunwale on to the sea. But when he let go his hold of the boat, and began to look about him, and saw how the wind was tearing the water, and how it tossed and raved between him and Jesus, he began to be afraid. And as soon as he began to be afraid he began to sink; but he had, notwithstanding his fear, just sense enough to do the one sensible thing; he cried out, 'Lord, save me.' And Jesus put out his hand, and took hold of him, and lifted him up out of the water, and said to him, 'O thou of little faith, wherefore didst thou doubt? And then they got into the boat, and the wind fell all at once, and altogether.

"Now, you will not think that Peter was a coward, will you? It wasn't that he hadn't courage, but that he hadn't enough of it. And why was it that he hadn't enough of it? Because he hadn't faith enough. Peter was always very easily impressed with the look of things. It wasn't at all likely that a man should be able to walk on the water; and yet Peter found himself standing on the water: you would have thought that when once he found himself standing on the water, he need not be afraid of the wind and the waves that lay between him and Jesus. But they looked so ugly that the fearfulness of them took hold of his heart, and his courage went. You would have thought that the greatest trial of his courage was over when he got out of the boat, and that there was comparatively little more ahead of him. Yet the sight of the waves and the blast of the boisterous wind were too much for him. I will tell you how I fancy it was; and I think there are several instances of the same kind of thing in Peter's life. When he got out of the boat, and found himself standing on the water, he began to think much of himself for being able to do so, and fancy himself better and greater than his companions, and an especial favourite of God above them. Now, there is nothing that kills faith sooner than pride. The two are directly against each other. The moment that Peter grew proud, and began to think about himself instead of about his Master, he began to lose his faith, and then he grew afraid, and then he began to sink—and that brought him to his senses. Then he forgot himself and remembered his Master, and then the hand of the Lord caught him, and the voice of the Lord gently rebuked him for the smallness of his faith, asking, 'Wherefore didst thou doubt?' I wonder if Peter was able to read his own heart sufficiently well to answer that **wherefore**. I do not think it likely at this period of his history. But God has immeasurable patience, and before he had done teaching Peter, even in this life, he had made him know quite well that pride and conceit were at the root of all his failures. Jesus did not point it out to him now. Faith was the only thing that would reveal that to him, as well as cure him of it; and was, therefore, the only thing he required of him in his rebuke. I suspect Peter was helped back into the boat by the eager hands of his companions already in a humbler state of mind than when he left it; but before his pride would be quite overcome, it would need that same voice of loving-kindness to call him Satan, and the voice of the cock to bring to his mind his loud boast, and his sneaking denial; nay, even the voice of one who had never seen the Lord till after his death, but was yet a readier disciple than he—the voice of St. Paul, to rebuke him because he dissembled, and was not downright honest. But at the last even he gained the crown of martyrdom, enduring all extremes, nailed to the cross like his Master, rather than deny his name. This should teach us to distrust ourselves, and yet have great hope for ourselves, and endless patience with other people. But to return to the story and what the story itself teaches us.

"If the disciples had known that Jesus saw them from the top of the mountain, and was watching them all the time, would they have been frightened at the storm, as I have little doubt they were, for they were only fresh-water fishermen, you know? Well, to answer my own question"—*I went on in haste, for I saw one or two of the sailors with an audible answer hovering on their lips*—"I don't know that, as they then were, it would have made so much difference to them; for none of them had risen much above the look of the things nearest them yet. But supposing you, who know something about him, were alone on the sea, and expecting your boat to be swamped every moment—if you found out all at once, that he was looking down at you from some lofty hilltop, and seeing all round about you in time and space too, would you be afraid? He might mean you to go to the bottom, you know. Would you mind going to the bottom with him looking at you? I do not think I should mind it myself. But I must take care lest I be boastful like Peter.

"Why should we be afraid of anything with him looking at us who is the Saviour of men? But we are afraid of him instead, because we do not believe that he is what he says he is—the Saviour of men. We do not believe what he offers us is salvation. We think it is slavery, and therefore continue slaves. Friends, I will speak to you who think you do believe in him. I am not going to say that you do not believe in him; but I hope I am going to make you say to yourselves that you too deserve to have those words of the Saviour spoken to you that were spoken to Peter, 'O ye of little faith!' Floating on the sea of your troubles, all kinds of fears and anxieties assailing you, is He not on the mountain-top? Sees he not the little boat of your fortunes tossed with the waves and the contrary wind? Assuredly he will come to you walking on the waters. It may not be in the way you wish, but if not, you will say at last, 'This is better.' It may be that he will come in a form that will make you cry out for fear in the weakness of your faith, as the disciples cried out—not believing any more than they did, that it can be he. But will not each of you arouse his courage that to you also he may say, as to the woman with the sick daughter whose confidence he so sorely tried, 'Great is thy faith'? Will you not rouse yourself, I say, that you may do him justice, and cast off the slavery of your own dread? O ye of little faith, wherefore will ye doubt? Do not think that the Lord sees and will not come. Down the mountain assuredly he will come, and you are now as safe in your troubles as the disciples were in theirs with Jesus looking on. They did not know it, but it was so: the Lord was watching them. And when you look back upon your past lives, cannot you see some instances of the same kind—when you felt and acted as if the Lord had forgotten you, and found afterwards that he had been watching you all the time?

"But the reason why you do not trust him more is that you obey him so little. If you would only, ask what God would have you to do, you would soon find your confidence growing. It is because you are proud, and envious, and greedy after gain, that you do not trust him more. Ah! trust him if it were only to get rid of these evil things, and be clean and beautiful in heart.

"O sailors with me on the ocean of life, will you, knowing that he is watching you from his mountain-top, do and say the things that hurt, and wrong, and disappoint him? Sailors on the waters that surround this globe, though there be no great mountain that overlooks the little lake on which you float, not the less does he behold you, and care for you, and watch over you. Will you do that which is unpleasing, distressful to him? Will you be irreverent, cruel, coarse? Will you say evil things, lie, and delight in vile stories and reports, with his eye on you, watching your ship on its watery ways, ever ready to come over the waves to help you? It is a fine thing, sailors, to fear nothing; but it would be far finer to fear nothing *because* he is above all, and over all, and in you all. For his sake and for his love, give up everything bad, and take him for your captain. He will be both captain and pilot to you, and steer you safe into the port of glory. Now to God the Father," &c. [pp. 211-222]

"The Harvest"

By this time the thanksgiving for the harvest was at hand: on the morning of that first of all would I summon the folk to their prayers with the sound of the full peal. And I wrote a little hymn of praise to the God of the harvest, modelling it to one of the oldest tunes in that part of the country, and I had it printed on slips of paper and laid plentifully on the benches. What with the calling of the bells, like voices in the highway, and the solemn meditation of the organ within to bear aloft the thoughts of those who heard, and came to the prayer and thanksgiving in common, and the message which God had given me to utter to them, I hoped that we should indeed keep holiday.

Wynnie summoned the parish with the hundredth psalm pealed from aloft, dropping from the airy regions of the tower on village and hamlet and cottage, calling aloud—for who could dissociate the words from the music, though the words are in the Scotch psalms?—written none the less by an Englishman, however English wits may amuse themselves with laughing at their quaintness— calling aloud,

> "All people that on earth do dwell
> Sing to the Lord with cheerful voice;
> Him serve with mirth, his praise forth tell—
> Come ye before him and rejoice."

Then we sang the psalm before the communion service, making bold in the name of the Lord to serve him with mirth as in the old version, and not with the fear with which some editor, weak in faith, has presumed to alter the line. Then before the sermon we sang the hymn I had prepared—a proceeding justifiable by many an example in the history of the church while she was not only able to number singers amongst her clergy, but those singers were capable of influencing the whole heart and judgment of the nation with their songs. Ethelwyn played the organ. The song I had prepared was this:

> "We praise the Life of All;
> From buried seeds so small
> Who makes the ordered ranks of autumn stand;
> Who stores the corn
> In rick and barn
> To feed the winter of the land.
> We praise the Life of Light!
> Who from the brooding night
> Draws out the morning holy, calm, and grand;
> Veils up the moon,
> Sends out the sun,
> To glad the face of all the land.
> We praise the Life of Work,
> Who from sleep's lonely dark
> Leads forth his children to arise and stand,
> Then go their way,
> The live-long day,
> To trust and labour in the land.
> We praise the Life of Good,
> Who breaks sin's lazy mood,
> Toilsomely ploughing up the fruitless sand.

The furrowed waste
They leave, and haste
Home, home, to till their Father's land.
We praise the Life of Life,
Who in this soil of strife
Casts us at birth, like seed from sower's hand;
To die and so
Like corn to grow
A golden harvest in his land."

After we had sung this hymn, the meaning of which is far better than the versification, I preached from the words of St. Paul, "If by any means I might attain unto the resurrection of the dead. Not as though I had already attained, either were already perfect." And this is something like what I said to them:

"The world, my friends, is full of resurrections, and it is not always of the same resurrection that St. Paul speaks. Every night that folds us up in darkness is a death; and those of you that have been out early and have seen the first of the dawn, will know it—the day rises out of the night like a being that has burst its tomb and escaped into life. That you may feel that the sunrise is a resurrection—the word resurrection just means a rising again—I will read you a little description of it from a sermon by a great writer and great preacher called Jeremy Taylor. Listen. 'But as when the sun approaching towards the gates of the morning, he first opens a little eye of heaven and sends away the spirits of darkness, and gives light to a cock, and calls up the lark to matins, and by and by gilds the fringes of a cloud, and peeps over the eastern hills, thrusting out his golden horns like those which decked the brows of Moses, when he was forced to wear a veil, because himself had seen the face of God; and still, while a man tells the story, the sun gets up higher, till he shows a fair face and a full light, and then he shines one whole day, under a cloud often, and sometimes weeping great and little showers, and sets quickly; so is a man's reason and his life.' Is not this a resurrection of the day out of the night? Or hear how Milton makes his Adam and Eve praise God in the morning,—

'Ye mists and exhalations that now rise
From hill or streaming lake, dusky or gray,

Till the sun paint your fleecy skirts with gold,
In honour to the world's great Author rise,
Whether to deck with clouds the uncoloured sky,
Or wet the thirsty earth with falling showers,
Rising or falling still advance his praise.'

But it is yet more of a resurrection to you. Think of your own condition through the night and in the morning. You die, as it were, every night. The death of darkness comes down over the earth; but a deeper death, the death of sleep, descends on you. A power overshadows you; your eyelids close, you cannot keep them open if you would; your limbs lie moveless; the day is gone; your whole life is gone; you have forgotten everything; an evil man might come and do with your goods as he pleased; you are helpless. But the God of the Resurrection is awake all the time, watching his sleeping men and women, even as a mother who watches her sleeping baby, only with larger eyes and more full of love than hers; and so, you know not how, all at once you know that you are what you are; that there is a world that wants you outside of you, and a God that wants you inside of you; you rise from the death of sleep, not by your own power, for you knew nothing about it; God put his hand over your eyes, and you were dead; he lifted his hand and breathed light on you and you rose from the dead, thanked the God who raised you up, and went forth to do your work. From darkness to light; from blindness to seeing; from knowing nothing to looking abroad on the mighty world; from helpless submission to willing obedience,—is not this a resurrection indeed? That St. Paul saw it to be such may be shown from his using the two things with the same meaning when he says, 'Awake, thou that sleepest, and arise from the dead, and Christ shall give thee light.' No doubt he meant a great deal more. No man who understands what he is speaking about can well mean only one thing at a time.

"But to return to the resurrections we see around us in nature. Look at the death that falls upon the world in winter. And look how it revives when the sun draws near enough in the spring to wile the life in it once more out of its grave. See how the pale, meek snowdrops come up with their bowed heads, as if full of the memory of the fierce winds they encountered last spring, and yet ready in the strength of their weakness to encounter them again. Up comes the crocus, bringing its gold safe from the dark of its colourless grave into the light of its parent gold. Primroses, and anemones, and blue-bells, and a thousand other children of the spring, hear the resurrection-trumpet of the wind from the west and south, obey, and leave their graves behind to breathe the air of the sweet heavens. Up and up they come till the year is glorious with the rose and the lily, till the trees are not only clothed upon with new garments of loveliest green, but the fruit-tree bringeth forth its fruit, and the little children of men are made glad with apples, and cherries, and hazel-nuts. The earth laughs out in green and gold. The sky shares in the grand resurrection. The garments of its mourning, wherewith it made men sad, its clouds of snow and hail and stormy vapours, are swept away, have sunk indeed to the earth, and are now humbly feeding the roots of the flowers whose dead stalks they beat upon all the winter long. Instead, the sky has put on the garments of praise. Her blue, coloured after the sapphire-floor on which stands the throne of him who is the Resurrection and the Life, is dashed and glorified with the pure white of sailing clouds, and at morning and evening prayer, puts on colours in which the human heart drowns itself with delight—green and gold and purple and rose. Even the icebergs floating about in the lonely summer seas of the north are flashing all the glories of the rainbow. But, indeed, is not this whole world itself a monument of the Resurrection? The earth was without form and void. The wind of God moved on the face of the waters, and up arose this fair world. Darkness was on the face of the deep: God said, 'Let there be light,' and there was light.

"In the animal world as well, you behold the goings of the Resurrection. Plainest of all, look at the story of the butterfly—so plain that the pagan Greeks called it and the soul by one name—Psyche. Psyche meant with them a butterfly or the soul, either. Look how the creeping thing, ugly to our eyes, so that we can hardly handle it without a shudder, finding itself growing sick with age, straightway falls a spinning and weaving at its own shroud, coffin, and grave, all in one—to prepare, in fact, for its resurrection; for it is for the sake of the resurrection that death exists. Patiently it spins its strength, but not its life, away, folds itself up decently, that its body may rest in quiet till the new body is formed within it; and at length when the appointed hour has arrived, out of the body of this crawling thing breaks forth the winged splendour of the butterfly—not the same body—a new one built out of the ruins of the old— even as St. Paul tells us that it is not the same body *we* have in the resurrection, but a nobler body like ourselves, with all the imperfect and evil thing taken away. No more creeping for the butterfly; wings of splendour now. Neither yet has it lost the feet wherewith to alight on all that is lovely and sweet. Think of it—up from the toilsome journey over the low ground, exposed to the foot of every passer-by, destroying the lovely leaves upon which it fed, and the fruit which they should shelter, up to the path at will through the air, and a gathering of food which hurts not the source of it, a food which is but as a tribute from the loveliness of the flowers to the yet higher loveliness of the flower-angel: is not this a resurrection? Its children too shall pass through the same process, to wing the air of a summer noon, and rejoice in the ethereal and the pure.

"To return yet again from the human thoughts suggested by the symbol of the butterfly"—

... "I come now naturally to speak of what we commonly call the Resurrection. Some say: 'How can the same dust be raised again, when it may be scattered to the winds of heaven?' It is a question I hardly care to answer. The mere difficulty can in reason stand for nothing with God; but the apparent worthlessness of the supposition renders the question uninteresting to me. What is of import is, that I should stand clothed upon, with a body which is *my* body because it serves my ends, justifies my consciousness of identity by being, in all that was good in it, like that which I had before, while now it is tenfold capable of expressing the thoughts and feelings that move within me. How can I care whether the atoms that form a certain inch of bone should be the same as those which formed that bone when I died? All my life-time I never felt or thought of the existence of such a bone! On the other hand, I object to having the same worn muscles, the same shrivelled skin with which I may happen to die. Why give me the same body as that? Why not rather my youthful body, which was strong, and facile, and capable? The matter in the muscle of my arm at death would not serve to make half the muscle I had when young. But I thank God that St. Paul says it will *not* be the same body. That body dies—up springs another body. I suspect myself that those are right who say that this body being the seed, the moment it dies in the soil of this world, that moment is the resurrection of the new body. The life in it rises out of it in a new body. This is not after it is put in the mere earth; for it is dead then, and the germ of life gone out of it. If a seed rots, no new body comes of it. The seed dies into a new life, and so does man. Dying and rotting are two very different things.—But I am not sure by any means. As I say, the whole question is rather uninteresting to me. What do I care about my old clothes after I have done with them? What is it to me to know what becomes of an old coat or an old pulpit gown? I have no such clinging to the flesh. It seems to me that people believe their bodies to be themselves, and are therefore very anxious about them—and no wonder then. Enough for me that I shall have eyes to see my friends, a face that they shall know me by, and a mouth to praise God withal. I leave the matter with one remark, that I am well content to rise as Jesus rose, however that was. For me the will of God is so good that I would rather have his will done than my own choice given me.

"But I now come to the last, because infinitely the most important part of my subject—the resurrection for the sake of which all the other resurrections exist—the resurrection unto Life. This is the one of which St. Paul speaks in my text. This is the one I am most anxious—indeed, the only one I am anxious to set forth, and impress upon you.

"Think, then, of all the deaths you know; the death of the night, when the sun is gone, when friend says not a word to friend, but both lie drowned and parted in the sea of sleep; the death of the year, when winter lies heavy on the graves of the children of summer, when the leafless trees moan in the blasts from the ocean, when the beasts even look dull and oppressed, when the children go about shivering with cold, when the poor and improvident are miserable with suffering or think of such a death of disease as befalls us at times, when the man who says, 'Would God it were morning!' changes but his word, and not his tune, when the morning comes, crying, 'Would God it were evening!' when what life is left is known to us only by suffering, and hope is amongst the things that were once and are no more—think of all these, think of them all together, and you will have but the dimmest, faintest picture of the death from which the resurrection of which I have now to speak, is the rising. I shrink from the attempt, knowing how weak words are to set forth *the* death, set forth *the* resurrection. Were I to sit down to yonder organ, and crash out the most horrible dissonances that ever took shape in sound, I should give you but a weak figure of this death; were I capable of drawing from many a row of pipes an exhalation of dulcet symphonies and voices sweet, such as Milton himself could have invaded our ears withal, I could give you but a faint figure of this resurrection. Nevertheless, I must try what I can do in my own way.

"If into the face of the dead body, lying on the bed, waiting for its burial, the soul of the man should begin to dawn again, drawing near from afar to look out once more at those eyes, to smile once again through those lips, the change on that face would be indeed great and wondrous, but nothing for marvel or greatness to that which passes on the countenance, the very outward bodily face of the man who wakes from his sleep, arises from the dead and receives light from Christ. Too often indeed, the reposeful look on the face of the dead body would be troubled, would vanish away at the revisiting of the restless ghost; but when a man's own right true mind, which God made in him, is restored to him again, and he wakes from the death of sin, then comes the repose without the death. It may take long for the new spirit to complete the visible change, but it begins at once, and will be perfected. The bloated look of self-indulgence passes away like the leprosy of Naaman, the cheek grows pure, the lips return to the smile of hope instead of the grin of greed, and the eyes that made innocence shrink and shudder with their yellow leer grow childlike and sweet and faithful. The mammon-eyes, hitherto fixed on the earth, are lifted to meet their kind; the lips that mumbled over figures and sums of gold learn to say words of grace and tenderness. The truculent, repellent, self-satisfied face begins to look thoughtful and doubtful, as if searching for some treasure of whose whereabouts it had no certain sign. The face anxious, wrinkled, peering, troubled, on whose lines you read the dread of hunger, poverty, and nakedness, thaws into a smile; the eyes reflect in courage the light of the Father's care, the back grows erect under its burden with the assurance that the hairs of its head are all numbered. But the face can with all its changes set but dimly forth the rising from the dead which passes within. The heart, which cared but for itself, becomes aware of surrounding thousands like itself, in the love and care of which it feels a dawning blessedness undreamt of before. From selfishness to love—is not this a rising from the dead? The man whose ambition declares that his way in the world would be to subject everything to his desires, to bring every human care, affection, power, and aspiration to his feet—such a world it would be, and such a king it would have, if individual ambition might work its will! if a man's opinion of himself could be made out in the world, degrading, compelling, oppressing, doing everything for his own glory!—and such a glory!—but a pang of light strikes this man to the heart; an arrow of truth, feathered with suffering and loss and dismay, finds out—the open joint in his armour, I was going to say—no, finds out the joint in the coffin where his heart lies festering in a death so dead that itself calls it life. He trembles, he awakes, he rises from the dead. No more he seeks the slavery of all: where can he find whom to serve? how can he become if but a threshold in the temple of Christ, where all serve all, and no man thinks first of himself? He to whom the mass of his fellows, as he massed them, was common and unclean, bows before every human sign of the presence of the making God. The sun, which was to him but a candle with which to search after his own ends, wealth, power, place, praise—the world, which was but the cavern where he thus searched—are now full of the mystery of loveliness, full of the truth of which sun and wind and land and sea are symbols and signs. From a withered old age of unbelief, the dim eyes of which refuse the glory of things a passage to the heart, he is raised up a child full of admiration, wonder, and gladness. Everything is glorious to him; he can believe, and therefore he sees. It is from the grave into the sunshine, from the night into the morning, from death into life. To come out of the ugly into the beautiful; out of the mean and selfish into the noble and loving; out of the paltry into the great; out of the false into the true; out of the filthy into the clean; out of the commonplace into the glorious; out of the corruption of disease into the fine vigour and gracious movements of health; in a word, out of evil into good—is not this a resurrection indeed—*the* resurrection of all, the resurrection of Life? God grant that with St. Paul we may attain to this resurrection of the dead.

"This rising from the dead is often a long and a painful process. Even after he had preached the gospel to the Gentiles, and suffered much for the sake of his Master, Paul sees the resurrection of the dead towering grandly before him, not yet climbed, not yet attained unto—a mountainous splendour and marvel, still shining aloft in the air of existence, still, thank God, to be attained, but ever growing in height and beauty as, forgetting those things that are behind, he presses towards the mark, if by any means he may attain to the resurrection of the dead. Every blessed moment in which a man bethinks himself that he has been forgetting his high calling, and sends up to the Father a prayer for aid; every time a man resolves that what he has been doing he will do no more; every time that the love of God, or the feeling of the truth, rouses a man to look first up at the light, then down at the skirts of his own garments—that moment a divine resurrection is wrought in the earth. Yea, every time that a man passes from resentment to forgiveness, from cruelty to compassion, from hardness to tenderness, from indifference to carefulness, from selfishness to honesty, from honesty to generosity, from generosity to love,— a resurrection, the bursting of a fresh bud of life out of the grave of evil, gladdens the eye of the Father watching his children. Awake, then, thou that sleepest, and arise from the dead, and Christ will give thee light. As the harvest rises from the wintry earth, so rise thou up from the trials of this world a full ear in the harvest of Him who sowed thee in the soil that thou mightest rise above it. As the summer rises from the winter, so rise thou from the cares of eating and drinking and clothing into the fearless sunshine of confidence in the Father. As the morning rises out of the night, so rise thou from the darkness of ignorance to do the will of God in the daylight; and as a man feels that he is himself when he wakes from the troubled and grotesque visions of the night into the glory of the sunrise, even so wilt thou feel that then first thou knowest what thy life, the gladness of thy being, is. As from painful tossing in disease, rise into the health of well-being. As from the awful embrace of thy own dead body, burst forth in thy spiritual body. Arise thou, responsive to the indwelling will of the Father, even as thy body will respond to thy indwelling soul.

> 'White wings are crossing;
> Glad waves are tossing;
> The earth flames out in crimson and green:
> Spring is appearing,
> Summer is nearing—
> Where hast thou been?
> Down in some cavern,
> Death's sleepy tavern,
> Housing, carousing with spectres of night?
> The trumpet is pealing
> Sunshine and healing—
> Spring to the light.'"

With this quotation from a friend's poem, I closed my sermon, oppressed with a sense of failure; for ever the marvel of simple awaking, the mere type of the resurrection eluded all my efforts to fix it in words. I had to comfort myself with the thought that God is so strong that he can work even with our failures. [pp. 407-422]

"THE SERMON"

When I stood up to preach, I gave them no text; but, with the eleventh chapter of the Gospel of St. John open before me, to keep me correct, I proceeded to tell the story in the words God gave me; for who can dare to say that he makes his own commonest speech?

"When Jesus Christ, the Son of God, and therefore our elder brother, was going about on the earth, eating and drinking with his brothers and sisters, there was one family he loved especially—a family of two sisters and a brother; for, although he loves everybody as much as they can be loved, there are some who can be loved more than others. Only God is always trying to make us such that we can be loved more and more. There are several stories—O, such lovely stories!—about that family and Jesus; and we have to do with one of them now.

"They lived near the capital of the country, Jerusalem, in a village they called Bethany; and it must have been a great relief to our Lord, when he was worn out with the obstinacy and pride of the great men of the city, to go out to the quiet little town and into the refuge of Lazarus's house, where everyone was more glad at the sound of his feet than at any news that could come to them.

"They had at this time behaved so ill to him in Jerusalem— taking up stones to stone him even, though they dared not quite do it, mad with anger as they were—and all because he told them the truth—that he had gone away to the other side of the great river that divided the country, and taught the people in that quiet place. While he was there his friend Lazarus was taken ill; and the two sisters, Martha and Mary, sent a messenger to him, to say to him, 'Lord, your friend is very ill.' Only they said it more beautifully than that: 'Lord, behold, he whom thou lovest is sick.' You know, when anyone is ill, we always want the person whom he loves most to come to him. This is very wonderful. In the worst things that can come to us the first thought is of love. People, like the Scribes and Pharisees, might say, 'What good can that do him?' And we may not in the least suppose that the person we want knows any secret that can cure his pain; yet love is the first thing we think of. And here we are more right than we know; for, at the long last, love will cure everything: which truth, indeed, this story will set forth to us. No doubt the heart of Lazarus, ill as he was, longed after his friend; and, very likely, even the sight of Jesus might have given him such strength that the life in him could have driven out the death which had already got one foot across the threshold. But the sisters expected more than this: they believed that Jesus, whom they knew to have driven disease and death out of so many hearts, had only to come and touch him—nay, only to speak a word, to look at him, and their brother was saved. Do you think they presumed in thus expecting? The fact was, they did not believe enough; they had not yet learned to believe that he could cure him all the same whether he came to them or not, because he was always with them. We cannot understand this; but our understanding is never a measure of what is true.

"Whether Jesus knew exactly all that was going to take place I cannot tell. Some people may feel certain upon points that I dare not feel certain upon. One thing I am sure of: that he did not always know everything beforehand, for he said so himself. It is infinitely more valuable to us, because more beautiful and godlike in him, that he should trust his Father than that he should foresee everything. At all events he knew that his Father did not want him to go to his friends yet. So he sent them a message to the effect that there was a particular reason for this sickness—that the end of it was not the death of Lazarus, but the glory of God. This, I think, he told them by the same messenger they sent to him; and then, instead of going to them, he remained where he was.

"But O, my friends, what shall I say about this wonderful message? Think of being sick for the glory of God! of being shipwrecked for the glory of God! of being drowned for the glory of God! How can the sickness, the fear, the broken-heartedness of his creatures be for the glory of God? What kind of a God can that be? Why just a God so perfectly, absolutely good, that the things that look least like it are only the means of clearing our eyes to let us see how good he is. For he is so good that he is not satisfied with *being* good. He loves his children, so that except he can make them good like himself, make them blessed by seeing how good he is, and desiring the same goodness in themselves, he is not satisfied. He is not like a fine proud benefactor, who is content with doing that which will satisfy his sense of his own glory, but like a mother who puts her arm round her child, and whose heart is sore till she can make her child see the love which is her glory. The glorification of the Son of God is the glorification of the human race; for the glory of God is the glory of man, and that glory is love. Welcome sickness, welcome sorrow, welcome death, revealing that glory!

"The next two verses sound very strangely together, and yet they almost seem typical of all the perplexities of God's dealings. The old painters and poets represented Faith as a beautiful woman, holding in her hand a cup of wine and water, with a serpent coiled up within. Highhearted Faith! she scruples not to drink of the life-giving wine and water; she is not repelled by the upcoiled serpent. The serpent she takes but for the type of the eternal wisdom that looks repellent because it is not understood. The wine is good, the water is good; and if the hand of the supreme Fate put that cup in her hand, the serpent itself must be good too,—harmless, at least, to hurt the truth of the water and the wine. But let us read the verses.

"Now Jesus loved Martha, and her sister, and Lazarus. When he had heard therefore that he was sick, he abode two days still in the same place where he was.'

"Strange! his friend was sick: he abode two days where he was! But remember what we have already heard. The glory of God was infinitely more for the final cure of a dying Lazarus, who, give him all the life he could have, would yet, without that glory, be in death, than the mere presence of the Son of God. I say *mere* presence, for, compared with the glory of God, the very presence of his Son, so dissociated, is nothing. He abode where he was that the glory of God, the final cure of humanity, the love that triumphs over death, might shine out and redeem the hearts of men, so that death could not touch them.

"After the two days, the hour had arrived. He said to his disciples, 'Let us go back to Judaea.' They expostulated, because of the danger, saying, 'Master, the Jews of late sought to stone thee; and goest thou thither again?' The answer which he gave them I am not sure whether I can thoroughly understand; but I think, in fact I know, it must bear on the same region of life—the will of God. I think what he means by walking in the day is simply doing the will of God. That was the sole, the all-embracing light in which Jesus ever walked. I think he means that now he saw plainly what the Father wanted him to do. If he did not see that the Father wanted him to go back to Judaea, and yet went, that would be to go stumblingly, to walk in the darkness. There are twelve hours in the day—one time to act— a time of light and the clear call of duty; there is a night when a man, not seeing where or hearing how, must be content to rest. Something not inharmonious with this, I think, he must have intended; but I do not see the whole thought clearly enough to be sure that I am right. I do think, further, that it points at a clearer condition of human vision and conviction than I am good enough to understand; though I hope one day to rise into this upper stratum of light.

"Whether his scholars had heard anything of Lazarus yet, I do not know. It looks a little as if Jesus had not told them the message he had had from the sisters. But he told them now that he was asleep, and that he was going to wake him. You would think they might have understood this. The idea of going so many miles to wake a man might have surely suggested death. But the disciples were sorely perplexed with many of his words. Sometimes they looked far away for the meaning when the meaning lay in their very hearts; sometimes they looked into their hands for it when it was lost in the grandeur of the ages. But he meant them to see into all that he said by and by, although they could not see into it now. When they understood him better, then they would understand what he said better. And to understand him better they must be more like him; and to make them more like him he must go away and give them his spirit—awful mystery which no man but himself can understand.

"Now he had to tell them plainly that Lazarus was dead. They had not thought of death as a sleep. I suppose this was altogether a new and Christian idea. Do not suppose that it applied more to Lazarus than to other dead people. He was none the less dead that Jesus meant to take a weary two days' journey to his sepulchre and wake him. If death is not a sleep, Jesus did not speak the truth when he said Lazarus slept. You may say it was a figure; but a figure that is not like the thing it figures is simply a lie.

"They set out to go back to Judaea. Here we have a glimpse of the faith of Thomas, the doubter. For a doubter is not without faith. The very fact that he doubts, shows that he has some faith. When I find anyone hard upon doubters, I always doubt the *quality* of his faith. It is of little use to have a great cable, if the hemp is so poor that it breaks like the painter of a boat. I have known people whose power of believing chiefly consisted in their incapacity for seeing difficulties. Of what fine sort a faith must be that is founded in stupidity, or far worse, in indifference to the truth and the mere desire to get out of hell! That is not a grand belief in the Son of God, the radiation of the Father. Thomas's want of faith was shown in the grumbling, self-pitying way in which he said, 'Let us also go that we may die with him.' His Master had said that he was going to wake him. Thomas said, 'that we may die with him.' You may say, 'He did not understand him.' True, it may be, but his unbelief was the cause of his not understanding him. I suppose Thomas meant this as a reproach to Jesus for putting them all in danger by going back to Judaea; if not, it was only a poor piece of sentimentality. So much for Thomas's unbelief. But he had good and true faith notwithstanding; for *he went with his Master.*

"By the time they reached the neighbourhood of Bethany, Lazarus had been dead four days. Someone ran to the house and told the sisters that Jesus was coming. Martha, as soon as she heard it, rose and went to meet him. It might be interesting at another time to compare the difference of the behaviour of the two sisters upon this occasion with the difference of their behaviour upon another occasion, likewise recorded; but with the man dead in his sepulchre, and the hope dead in these two hearts, we have no inclination to enter upon fine distinctions of character. Death and grief bring out the great family likenesses in the living as well as in the dead.

"When Martha came to Jesus, she showed her true though imperfect faith by almost attributing her brother's death to Jesus' absence. But even in the moment, looking in the face of the Master, a fresh hope, a new budding of faith, began in her soul. She thought—'What if, after all, he were to bring him to life again!' O, trusting heart, how thou leavest the dull-plodding intellect behind thee! While the conceited intellect is reasoning upon the impossibility of the thing, the expectant faith beholds it accomplished. Jesus, responding instantly to her faith, granting her half-born prayer, says, 'Thy brother shall rise again;' not meaning the general truth recognised, or at least assented to by all but the Sadducees, concerning the final resurrection of the dead, but meaning, 'Be it unto thee as thou wilt. I will raise him again.' For there is no steering for a fine effect in the words of Jesus. But these words are too good for

Martha to take them as he meant them. Her faith is not quite equal to the belief that he actually will do it. The thing she could hope for afar off she could hardly believe when it came to her very door. 'O, yes,' she said, her mood falling again to the level of the commonplace, 'of course, at the last day.' Then the Lord turns away her thoughts from the dogmas of her faith to himself, the Life, saying, 'I am the resurrection and the life: he that believeth in me, though he were dead, yet shall he live. And whosoever liveth and believeth in me, shall never die. Believest thou this?' Martha, without understanding what he said more than in a very poor part, answered in words which preserved her honesty entire, and yet included all he asked, and a thousandfold more than she could yet believe: 'Yea, Lord; I believe that thou art the Christ, the Son of God, which should come into the world.'

"I dare not pretend to have more than a grand glimmering of the truth of Jesus' words 'shall never die;' but I am pretty sure that when Martha came to die, she found that there was indeed no such thing as she had meant when she used the ghastly word *death*, and said with her first new breath, 'Verily, Lord, I am not dead.'

"But look how this declaration of her confidence in the Christ operated upon herself. She instantly thought of her sister; the hope that the Lord would do something swelled within her, and, leaving Jesus, she went to find Mary. Whoever has had a true word with the elder brother, straightway will look around him to find his brother, his sister. The family feeling blossoms: he wants his friend to share the glory withal. Martha wants Mary to go to Jesus too.

"Mary heard her, forgot her visitors, rose, and went. They thought she went to the grave: she went to meet its conqueror. But when she came to him, the woman who had chosen the good part praised of Jesus, had but the same words to embody her hope and her grief that her careful and troubled sister had uttered a few minutes before. How often during those four days had not the self-same words passed between them! 'Ah, if he had been here, our brother had not died!' She said so to himself now, and wept, and her friends who had followed her wept likewise. A moment more, and the Master groaned; yet a moment, and he too wept. 'Sorrow is catching;' but this was not the mere infection of sorrow. It went deeper than mere sympathy; for he groaned in his spirit and was troubled. What made him weep? It was when he saw them weeping that he wept. But why should he weep, when he knew how soon their weeping would be turned into rejoicing? It was not for their weeping, so soon to be over, that he wept, but for the human heart everywhere swollen with tears, yea, with griefs that can find no such relief as tears; for these, and for all his brothers and sisters tormented with pain for lack of faith in his Father in heaven, Jesus wept. He saw the blessed well-being of Lazarus on the one side, and on the other the streaming eyes from whose sight he had vanished. The veil between was so thin! yet the sight of those eyes could not pierce it: their hearts must go on weeping—without cause, for his Father was so good. I think it was the helplessness he felt in the impossibility of at once sweeping away the phantasm death from their imagination that drew the tears from the eyes of Jesus. Certainly it was not for Lazarus; it could hardly be for these his friends—save as they represented the humanity which he would help, but could not help even as he was about to help them.

"The Jews saw herein proof that he loved Lazarus; but they little thought it was for them and their people, and for the Gentiles whom they despised, that his tears were now flowing—that the love which pressed the fountains of his weeping was love for every human heart, from Adam on through the ages.

"Some of them went a little farther, nearly as far as the sisters, saying, 'Could he not have kept the man from dying?' But it was such a poor thing, after all, that they thought he might have done. They regarded merely this unexpected illness, this early death; for I daresay Lazarus was not much older than Jesus. They did not think that, after all, Lazarus must die some time; that the beloved could be saved, at best, only for a little while. Jesus seems to have heard the remark, for he again groaned in himself.

"Meantime they were drawing near the place where he was buried. It was a hollow in the face of a rock, with a stone laid against it. I suppose the bodies were laid on something like shelves inside the rock, as they are in many sepulchres. They were not put into coffins, but wound round and round with linen.

"When they came before the door of death, Jesus said to them, 'Take away the stone.' The nature of Martha's reply—the realism of it, as they would say now-a-days—would seem to indicate that her dawning faith had sunk again below the horizon, that in the presence of the insignia of death, her faith yielded, even as the faith of Peter failed him when he saw around him the grandeur of the high-priest, and his Master bound and helpless. Jesus answered—O, what an answer!—To meet the corruption and the stink which filled her poor human fancy, 'the glory of God' came from his lips: human fear; horror speaking from the lips of a woman in the very jaws of the devouring death; and the 'said I not unto thee?' from the mouth of him who was so soon to pass worn and bloodless through such a door! 'He stinketh,' said Martha. 'The glory of God,' said Jesus. 'Said I not unto thee, that, if thou wouldest believe, thou shouldest see the glory of God?'

"Before the open throat of the sepulchre Jesus began to speak to his Father aloud. He had prayed to him in his heart before, most likely while he groaned in his spirit. Now he thanked him that he had comforted him, and given him Lazarus as a first-fruit from the dead. But he will be true to the listening people as well as to his ever-hearing Father; therefore he tells why he said the word of thanks aloud—a thing not usual with him, for his Father was always hearing, him. Having spoken it for the people, he would say that it was for the people.

"The end of it all was that they might believe that God had sent him—a far grander gift than having the dearest brought back from the grave; for he is the life of men.

"'Lazarus, come forth!'

"And Lazarus came forth, creeping helplessly with inch-long steps of his linen-bound limbs. 'Ha, ha! brother, sister!' cries the human heart. The Lord of Life hath taken the prey from the spoiler; he hath emptied the grave. Here comes the dead man, welcome as never was child from the womb—new-born, and in him all the human race new-born from the grave! 'Loose him and let him go,' and the work is done. The sorrow is over, and the joy is come. Home, home, Martha, Mary, with your Lazarus! He too will go with you, the Lord of the Living. Home and get the feast ready, Martha! Prepare the food for him who comes hungry from the grave, for him who has called him thence. Home, Mary, to help Martha! What a household will yours be! What wondrous speech will pass between the dead come to life and the living come to die!

"But what pang is this that makes Lazarus draw hurried breath, and turns Martha's cheek so pale? Ah, at the little window of the heart the pale eyes of the defeated Horror look in. What! is he there still! Ah, yes, he will come for Martha, come for Mary, come yet again for Lazarus—yea, come for the Lord of Life himself, and carry all away. But look at the Lord: he knows all about it, and he smiles. Does Martha think of the words he spoke, 'He that liveth and believeth in me shall never die'? Perhaps she does, and, like the moon before the sun, her face returns the smile of her Lord.

"This, my friends, is a fancy in form, but it embodies a dear truth. What is it to you and me that he raised Lazarus? We are not called upon to believe that he will raise from the tomb that joy of our hearts which lies buried there beyond our sight. Stop! Are we not? We are called upon to believe this; else the whole story were for us a poor mockery. What is it to us that the Lord raised Lazarus?—Is it nothing to know that our Brother is Lord over the grave? Will the harvest be behind the first-fruits? If he tells us he cannot, for good reasons, raise up our vanished love to-day, or to-morrow, or for all the years of our life to come, shall we not mingle the smile of faithful thanks with the sorrow of present loss, and walk diligently waiting? That he called forth Lazarus showed that he was in his keeping, that he is Lord of the living, and that all live to him, that he has a hold of them, and can draw them forth when he will. If this is not true, then the raising of Lazarus is false; I do not mean merely false in fact, but false in meaning. If we believe in him, then in his name, both for ourselves and for our friends, we must deny death and believe in life. Lord Christ, fill our hearts with thy Life!" [pp. 578-591]

❖ CHAPTER 3 ❖

A "SERMON" FROM THE VICAR'S DAUGHTER

In the third book of the trilogy, the main character is Henry Walton's married daughter Wynnie Percival. It contains no sermon by Walton. In fact, it contains no actual sermon at all but instead a wonderful Socratic Bible study by Marion, a woman who works with poor people in London. Marion is based loosely on MacDonald's friend, the social worker Octavia Hill. Although it is not a sermon, it contains some of MacDonald's best comments on the problem of suffering. Wynnie, Walton's daughter, and her brother-in-law have just entered the room where Marion is conducting the Bible study.

"A STRANGE TEXT"

Before she had read many words, Roger and I began to cast strange looks on each other. For this was the chapter she read:—

"And Joseph, wheresoever he went in the city, took the Lord Jesus with him, where he was sent for to work, to make gates, or milk-pails, or sieves, or boxes; the Lord Jesus was with him wheresoever he went. And as often as Joseph had any thing in his work to make longer or shorter, or wider or narrower, the Lord Jesus would stretch his hand towards it. And presently it became as Joseph would have it. So that he had no need to finish any thing with his own hands, for he was not very skilful at his carpenter's trade.

"On a certain time the king of Jerusalem sent for him, and said, 'I would have thee make me a throne of the same dimensions with that place in which I commonly sit.' Joseph obeyed, and forthwith began the work, and continued two years in the king's palace before he finished. And when he came to fix it in its place, he found it wanted two spans on each side of the appointed measure. Which, when the king saw, he was very angry with Joseph; and Joseph, afraid of the king's anger, went to bed without his supper, taking not any thing to eat. Then the Lord Jesus asked him what he was afraid of. Joseph replied, 'Because I have lost my labor in the work which I have been about these two years.' Jesus said to him, Fear not, neither be cast down; do thou lay hold on one side of the throne, and I will the other, and we will bring it to its just dimensions.' And when Joseph had done as the Lord Jesus said, and each of them had with strength drawn his side, the throne obeyed, and was brought to the proper dimensions of the place; which miracle when they who stood by saw, they were astonished, and praised God. The throne was made of the same wood which was in being in Solomon's time, namely, wood adorned with various shapes and figures."

Her voice ceased, and a pause followed.

"We must go in now," I whispered.

"She'll be going to say something now; just wait till she's started," said Roger.

"Now, what do you think of it?" asked Marion in a meditative tone.

We crept within the scope of her vision, and stood. A voice, which I knew, was at the moment replying to her question.

"*I* don't think it's much of a chapter, that, grannie."

The speaker was the keen-faced, elderly man, with iron-gray whiskers. He sat near where we stood by the door, between two respectable looking women, who had been listening to the chapter as devoutly as if it had been of the true gospel.

"Sure, grannie, that ain't out o' the Bible?" said another voice, from somewhere farther off.

"We'll talk about that presently," answered Marion.

"I want to hear what Mr. Jarvis has to say to it: he's a carpenter himself, you see,—a joiner, that is, you know."

All the faces in the room were now turned towards Jarvis.

"Tell me why you don't think much of it, Mr. Jarvis," said Marion.

"Tain't a bit likely," he answered.

"What isn't likely?"

"Why, not one single thing in the whole kit of it. And first and foremost, 'tain't a bit likely the old man 'ud ha' been sich a duffer."

"Why not? There must have been stupid people then as well as now."

"Not *his* father." said Jarvis decidedly.

"He wasn't but his step-father, like, you know, Mr. Jarvis," remarked the woman beside him in a low voice.

"Well, he'd never ha' been *hers*, then. *She* wouldn't ha' had a word to say to *him*."

"I have seen a good—and wise woman too—with a dull husband," said Marion.

"You know you don't believe a word of it yourself, grannie," said still another voice.

"Besides," she went on without heeding the interruption, "in those times, I suspect, such things were mostly managed by the parents, and the woman herself had little to do with them."

A murmur of subdued indignation arose,—chiefly of female voices.

"Well, *they* wouldn't then," said Jarvis.

"He might have been rich," suggested Marion.

"I'll go bail *he* never made the money then," said Jarvis. "An old idget! I don't believe sich a feller 'ud ha' been *let* marry a woman like her—I *don't*."

"You mean you don't think God would have let him?"

"Well, that's what I *do* mean, grannie. The thing couldn't ha' been, nohow."

"I agree with you quite. And now I want to hear more of what in the story you don't consider likely."

"Well, it ain't likely sich a workman 'ud ha' stood so high i' the trade that the king of Jerusalem would ha' sent for *him* of all the tradesmen in the town to make his new throne for him. No more it ain't likely—and let him be as big a duffer as ever was, to be a jiner at all—that he'd ha' been two year at work on that there throne—an' a carvin' of it in figures too!—and never found out it was four spans too narrer for the place it had to stand in. Do ye 'appen to know now, grannie, how much is a span?"

"I don't know. Do you know, Mrs. Percivale?"

The sudden reference took me very much by surprise; but I had not forgotten, happily, the answer I received to the same question, when anxious to realize the monstrous height of Goliath.

"I remember my father telling me," I replied, "that it was as much as you could stretch between your thumb and little finger."

"There!" cried Jarvis triumphantly, parting the extreme members of his right hand against the back of the woman in front of him—"that would be seven or eight inches! Four times that? Two foot and a half at least! Think of that!"

"I admit the force of both your objections," said Marion. "And now, to turn to a more important part of the story, what do you think of the way in which according to it he got his father out of his evil plight?"

I saw plainly enough that she was quietly advancing towards some point in her view,—guiding the talk thitherward, steadily, without haste or effort.

Before Jarvis had time to make any reply, the blind man, mentioned in a former chapter, struck in, with the tone of one who had been watching his opportunity.

"*I* make more o' that pint than the t'other," he said. "A man as is a duffer may well make a mull of a thing; but a man as knows what he's up to can't. I don't make much o' them miracles, you know, grannie—that is, I don't know, and what I don't know, I won't say as I knows; but what I'm sure of is this here one thing,—that man or boy as *could* work a miracle, you know, grannie, wouldn't work no miracle as there wasn't no good working of."

"It was to help his father," suggested Marion.

Here Jarvis broke in almost with scorn.

"To help him to pass for a clever fellow, when he was as great a duffer as ever broke bread!"

"I'm quite o' your opinion, Mr. Jarvis," said the blind man. "It 'ud ha' been more like him to tell his father what a duffer he was, and send him home to learn his trade."

"He couldn't do that, you know," said Marion gently. "He *couldn't* use such words to his father, if he were ever so stupid."

"His step-father, grannie," suggested the woman who had corrected Jarvis on the same point. She spoke very modestly, but was clearly bent on holding forth what light she had.

"Certainly, Mrs. Renton; but you know he couldn't be rude to any one,—leaving his own mother's husband out of the question."

"True for you, grannie," returned the woman.

"I think, though," said Jarvis, "for as hard as he'd ha' found it, it would ha' been more like him to set to work and teach his father, than to scamp up his mulls."

"Certainly," acquiesced Marion. "To hide any man's faults, and leave him not only stupid, but, in all probability, obstinate and self-satisfied, would not be like *him*. Suppose our Lord had had such a father: what do you think he would have done?"

"He'd ha' done all he could to make a man of him," answered Jarvis.

"Wouldn't he have set about making him comfortable then, in spite of his blunders?" said Marion.

A significant silence followed this question.

"Well, *no*; not first thing, I don't think," returned Jarvis at length. "He'd ha' got him o' some good first, and gone in to make him comfortable arter."

"Then I suppose you would rather be of some good and uncomfortable, than of no good and comfortable?" said Marion.

"I hope so, grannie," answered Jarvis; and "*I* would;" "Yes;" "That I would," came from several voices in the little crowd, showing what an influence Marion must have already had upon them.

"Then," she said,—and I saw by the light which rose in her eyes that she was now coming to the point,—"Then, surely it must be worth our while to bear discomfort in order to grow of some good! Mr. Jarvis has truly said, that, if Jesus had had such a father, he would have made him of some good before he made him comfortable: that is just the way your Father in heaven is acting with you. Not many of you would say you are of much good yet; but you would like to be better. And yet,—put it to yourselves,—do you not grumble at every thing that comes to you that you don't like, and call it bad luck, and worse—yes, even when you know it comes of your own fault, and nobody else's? You think if you had only this or that to make you comfortable, you would be content; and you call it very hard that So-and-so should be getting on well, and saving money, and you down on your luck, as you say. Some of you even grumble that your neighbors' children should be healthy when yours are pining. You would allow that you are not of much good yet; but you forget that to make you comfortable as you are would be the same as to pull out Joseph's misfitted thrones and doors, and make his misshapen buckets over again for him. That you think so absurd that you can't believe the story a bit; but you would be helped out of all *your* troubles, even those you bring on yourselves, not thinking what the certain consequence would be, namely, that you would grow of less and less value, until you were of no good, either to God or man. If you think about it, you will see that I am right. When, for instance, are you most willing to do right? When are you most ready to hear about good things? When are you most inclined to pray to God? When you have plenty of money in your pockets, or when you are in want? when you have had a good dinner, or when you have not enough to get one? when you are in jolly health, or when the life seems ebbing out of you in misery and pain? No matter that you may have brought it on yourselves; it is no less God's way of bringing you back to him, for he decrees that suffering shall follow sin: it is just then you most need it; and, if it drives you to God, that is its end, and there will be an end of it. The prodigal was himself to blame for the want that made him a beggar at the swine's trough; yet that want was the greatest blessing God could give to him, for it drove him home to his father.

"But some of you will say you are no prodigals; nor is it your fault that you find yourselves in such difficulties that life seems hard to you. It would be very wrong in me to set myself up as your judge, and to tell you that it *was* your fault. If it is, God will let you know it. But if it be not your fault, it does not follow that you need the less to be driven back to God. It is not only in punishment of our sins that we are made to suffer: God's runaway children must be brought back to their home and their blessedness,—back to their Father in heaven. It is not always a sign that God is displeased with us when he makes us suffer. 'Whom the Lord loveth he chasteneth, and scourgeth every son whom he receiveth. If ye endure chastening, God dealeth with you as with sons.' But instead of talking more about it, I must take it to myself; and learn not to grumble when *my* plans fail."

"That's what *you* never goes and does, grannie," growled a voice from somewhere.

I learned afterwards it was that of a young tailor, who was constantly quarrelling with his mother.

"I think I have given up grumbling at my circumstances," she rejoined; "but then I have nothing to grumble at in them. I haven't known hunger or cold for a great many years now. But I do feel discontented at times when I see some of you not getting better so fast as I should like. I ought to have patience, remembering how patient God is with my conceit and stupidity, and not expect too much of you. Still, it can't be wrong to wish that you tried a good deal more to do what he wants of you. Why should his children not be his friends? If you would but give yourselves up to him, you would find his yoke so easy, his burden so light! But you do it half only, and some of you not at all.

"Now, however, that we have got a lesson from a false gospel, we may as well get one from the true."

As she spoke, she turned to her New Testament which lay

beside her. But Jarvis interrupted her.

"Where did you get that stuff you was a readin' of to us, grannie?" he asked.

"The chapter I read to you," she answered, "is part of a pretended gospel, called, 'The First Gospel of the Infancy of Jesus Christ.' I can't tell you who wrote it, or how it came to be written. All I can say is, that, very early in the history of the church, there were people who indulged themselves in inventing things about Jesus, and seemed to have had no idea of the importance of keeping to facts, or, in other words, of speaking and writing only the truth. All they seemed to have cared about was the gratifying of their own feelings of love and veneration; and so they made up tales about him, in his honor as they supposed, no doubt, just as if he had been a false god of the Greeks or Romans. It is long before some people learn to speak the truth, even after they know it is wicked to lie. Perhaps, however, they did not expect their stories to be received as facts, intending them only as a sort of recognized fiction about him,—amazing presumption at the best."

"Did anybody, then, ever believe the likes of that, grannie?" asked Jarvis.

"Yes: what I read to you seems to have been believed within a hundred years after the death of the apostles. There are several such writings, with a great deal of nonsense in them, which were generally accepted by Christian people for many hundreds of years."

"I can't imagine how anybody could go inwentuating such things!" said the blind man.

"It is hard for us to imagine. They could not have seen how their inventions would, in later times, be judged any thing but honoring to him in whose honor they wrote them. Nothing, be it ever so well invented, can be so good as the bare truth. Perhaps, however, no one in particular invented some of them, but the stories grew, just as a report often does amongst yourselves. Although everybody fancies he or she is only telling just what was told to him or her, yet, by degrees, the pin's-point of a fact is covered over with lies upon lies, almost everybody adding something, until the report has grown to be a mighty falsehood. Why, you had such a story yourselves, not so very long ago, about one of your best friends! One comfort is, such a story is sure not to be consistent with itself; it is sure to show its own falsehood to any one who is good enough to doubt it, and who will look into it, and examine it well. You don't, for instance, want any other proof than the things themselves to show you that what I have just read to you can't be true."

"But then it puzzles me to think how anybody could believe them," said the blind man.

"Many of the early Christians were so childishly simple that they would believe almost any thing that was told them. In a time when such nonsense could be written, it is no great wonder there should be many who could believe it."

"Then, what was their faith worth," said the blind man, "if they believed false and true all the same?"

"Worth no end to them," answered Marion with eagerness; "for all the false things they might believe about him could not destroy the true ones, or prevent them from believing in Jesus himself, and bettering their ways for his sake. And as they grew better and better, by doing what he told them, they would gradually come to disbelieve this and that foolish or bad thing."

"But wouldn't that make them stop believing in him altogether?"

"On the contrary, it would make them hold the firmer to all that they saw to be true about him. There are many people, I presume, in other countries, who believe those stories still; but all the Christians I know have cast aside every one of those writings, and keep only to those we call the Gospels. To throw away what is not true, because it is not true, will always help the heart to be truer; will make it the more anxious to cleave to what it sees must be true. Jesus remonstrated with the Jews that they would not of themselves judge what was right; and the man who lets God teach him is made abler to judge what is right a thousand-fold."

"Then don't you think it likely this much is true, grannie,"— said Jarvis, probably interested in the question, in part at least, from the fact that he was himself a carpenter,—"that he worked with his father, and helped him in his trade?"

"I do, indeed," answered Marion. "I believe that is the one germ of truth in the whole story. It is possible even that some incidents of that part of his life may have been handed down a little way, at length losing all their shape, however, and turning into the kind of thing I read to you. Not to mention that they called him the carpenter, is it likely he who came down for the express purpose of being a true man would see his father toiling to feed him and his mother and his brothers and sisters, and go idling about, instead of putting to his hand to help him? Would that have been like him?"

"Certainly not," said Mr. Jarvis.

But a doubtful murmur came from the blind man, which speedily took shape in the following remark:—

"I can't help thinkin', grannie, of one time—you read it to us not long ago—when he laid down in the boat and went fast asleep, takin' no more heed o' them a slavin' o' theirselves to death at their oars, than if they'd been all comfortable like hisself; that wasn't much like takin' of his share—was it now?"

"John Evans," returned Marion with severity, "it is quite right to put any number of questions, and express any number of doubts you honestly feel; but you have no right to make remarks you would not make if you were anxious to be as fair to another as you would have another be to you. Have you considered that he had been working hard all day long, and was, in fact, worn out? You don't think what hard work it is, and how exhausting, to speak for hours to great multitudes, and in the open air too, where your voice has no help to make it heard. And that's not all; for he had most likely been healing many as well; and I believe every time the power went out of him to cure, he suffered in the relief he gave; it left him weakened,—with so much the less of strength to support his labors,—so that, even in his very body, he took our iniquities and bare our infirmities. Would you, then, blame a weary man, whose perfect faith in God rendered it impossible for him to fear any thing, that he lay down to rest in God's name, and left his friends to do their part for the redemption of the world in rowing him to the other side of the lake,—a thing they were doing every other day of their lives? You ought to consider before you make such remarks, Mr. Evans. And you forget also that the moment they called him, he rose to help them."

"And find fault with them," interposed Evans, rather viciously I thought.

"Yes; for they were to blame for their own trouble, and ought to send it away."

"What! To blame for the storm? How could they send that away?"

"Was it the storm that troubled them then? It was their own fear of it. The storm could not have troubled them if they had had faith in their Father in heaven."

"They had good cause to be afraid of it, anyhow."

"He judged they had not, for he was not afraid himself. You judge they had, because you would have been afraid."

"He could help himself, you see."

"And they couldn't trust either him or his Father, notwithstanding all he had done to manifest himself and his Father to them. Therefore he saw that the storm about them was not the thing that most required rebuke."

"I never pretended to much o' the sort," growled Evans. "Quite the contrairy."

"And why? Because, like an honest man, you wouldn't pretend to what you hadn't got. But, if you carried your honesty far enough, you would have taken pains to understand our Lord first. Like his other judges, you condemn him beforehand. You will not call that honesty?"

"I don't see what right you've got to badger me like this before a congregation o' people," said the blind man, rising in indignation. "If I ain't got my heyesight, I ha' got my feelin's."

"And do you think *he* has no feelings, Mr. Evans? You have spoken evil of *him*: I have spoken but the truth of *you*!"

"Come, come, grannie," said the blind man, quailing a little; "don't talk squash. I'm a livin' man afore the heyes o' this here company, an' he ain't nowheres. Bless you, *he* don't mind!"

"He minds so much," returned Marion, in a subdued voice, which seemed to tremble with coming tears, "that he will never rest until you think fairly of him. And he is here now; for he said, 'I am with you alway, to the end of the world;' and he has heard every word you have been saying against him. He isn't angry like me; but your words may well make him feel sad—for your sake, John Evans—that you should be so unfair."

She leaned her forehead on her hand, and was silent. A subdued murmur arose. The blind man, having stood irresolute for a moment, began to make for the door, saying,—

"I think I'd better go. I ain't wanted here."

"If you *are* an honest man, Mr. Evans," returned Marion, rising, "you will sit down and hear the case out."

With a waving, fin-like motion of both his hands, Evans sank into his seat, and spoke no word.

After but a moment's silence, she resumed as if there had been no interruption.

"That he should sleep, then, during the storm was a very different thing from declining to assist his father in his workshop; just as the rebuking of the sea was a very different thing from hiding up his father's bad work in miracles. Had that father been in danger, he might perhaps have aided him as he did the disciples. But"—

"Why do you say *perhaps*, grannie?" interrupted a bright-eyed boy who sat on the hob of the empty grate. "Wouldn't he help his father as soon as his disciples?"

"Certainly, if it was good for his father; certainly not, if it was not good for him: therefore I say *perhaps*. But now," she went on, turning to the joiner, "Mr. Jarvis, will you tell me whether you think the work of the carpenter's son would have been in any way distinguishable from that of another man?"

"Well, I don't know, grannie. He wouldn't want to be putting of a private mark upon it. He wouldn't want to be showing of it off—would he? He'd use his tools like another man, anyhow."

"All that we may be certain of. He came to us a man, to live a man's life, and do a man's work. But just think a moment. I will put the question again: Do you suppose you would have been able to distinguish his work from that of any other man?"

A silence followed. Jarvis was thinking. He and the blind man were of the few that can think. At last his face brightened.

"Well, grannie," he said, "I think it would be very difficult in any thing easy, but very easy in any thing difficult."

He laughed,—for he had not perceived the paradox before uttering it.

"Explain yourself, if you please, Mr. Jarvis. I am not sure that I understand you," said Marion.

"I mean, that, in an easy job, which any fair workman could do well enough, it would not be easy to tell his work. But, where the job was difficult, it would be so much better done, that it would not be difficult to see the better hand in it."

"I understand you, then, to indicate, that the chief distinction would lie in the quality of the work; that whatever he did, he would do in such a thorough manner, that over the whole of what he turned out, as you would say, the perfection of the work would be a striking characteristic. Is that it?"

"That is what I do mean, grannie."

"And that is just the conclusion I had come to myself."

"*I* should like to say just one word to it, grannie, so be you won't cut up crusty," said the blind man.

"If you are fair, I sha'n't be crusty, Mr. Evans. At least, I hope not," said Marion.

"Well, it's this: Mr. Jarvis he say as how the jiner-work done by Jesus Christ would be better done than e'er another man's,— tip-top fashion,—and there would lie the differ. Now, it do seem to me as I've got no call to come to that 'ere conclusion. You been tellin' on us, grannie, I donno how long now, as how Jesus Christ was the Son of God, and that he come to do the works of God,—down here like, afore our faces, that we might see God at work, by way of. Now, I ha' nothin' to say agin that: it may be, or it mayn't be—I can't tell. But if that be the way on it, then I don't see how Mr. Jarvis can be right; the two don't curryspond,—not by no means. For the works o' God—there ain't one on'em as I can see downright well managed—tip-top jiner's work, as I may say; leastways,—Now stop a bit, grannie; don't trip a man up, and then say as he fell over his own dog,—leastways, I don't say about the moon an' the stars an' that; I dessay the sun he do get up the werry moment he's called of a mornin', an' the moon when she ought to for her night-work,—I ain't no 'stronomer strawnry, and I ain't heerd no complaints about *them*; but I do say as how, down here, we ha' got most uncommon bad weather more'n at times; and the walnuts they turns out, every now an' then, full o' mere dirt; an' the oranges awful. There 'ain't been a good crop o' hay, they tells me, for many's the year. An' i' furren parts, what wi' earthquakes an' wolcanies an' lions an' tigers, an' savages as eats their wisiters, an' chimley-pots blowin' about, an' ships goin' down, an' fathers o' families choked an' drownded an' burnt i' coal-pits by the hundred,—it do seem to me that if his jinerin' hadn't been tip-top, it would ha' been but like the rest on it. There, grannie! Mind, I mean no offence; an' I don't doubt you ha' got somethink i' your weskit pocket as 'll turn it all topsy-turvy in a moment. Anyhow, I won't purtend to nothink, and that's how it look to me."

"I admit," said Marion, "that the objection is a reasonable one. But why do you put it, Mr. Evans, in such a triumphant way, as if you were rejoiced to think it admitted of no answer, and believed the world would be ever so much better off if the storms and the tigers had it all their own way, and there were no God to look after things."

"Now, you ain't fair to *me*, grannie. Not avin' of my heyesight like the rest on ye, I may be a bit fond of a harguyment; but I tries to hit fair, and when I hears what ain't logic, I can no more help comin' down upon it than I can help breathin' the air o' heaven. And why shouldn't I? There ain't no law agin a harguyment. An' more an' over, it do seem to me as how you and Mr. Jarvis is wrong i' *it is* harguyment."

"If I was too sharp upon you, Mr. Evans, and I may have been," said Marion, "I beg your pardon."

"It's granted, grannie."

"I don't mean, you know, that I give in to what you say,—not one bit."

"I didn't expect it of you. I'm a-waitin' here for you to knock me down."

"I don't think a mere victory is worth the breath spent upon it," said Marion. "But we should all be glad to get or give more light upon any subject, if it be by losing ever so many arguments. Allow me just to put a question or two to Mr. Jarvis, because he's a joiner himself—and that's a great comfort to me to-night: What would you say, Mr. Jarvis, of a master who planed the timber he used for scaffolding, and tied the crosspieces with ropes of silk?"

"I should say he was a fool, grannie,—not only for losin' of his money and his labor, but for weakenin' of his scaffoldin',—summat like the old throne-maker i' that chapter, I should say."

"What's the object of a scaffold, Mr. Jarvis?"

"To get at something else by means of,—say build a house."

"Then, so long as the house was going up all right, the probability is there wouldn't be much amiss with the scaffold?"

"Certainly, provided it stood till it was taken down."

"And now, Mr. Evans," she said next, turning to the blind man, "I am going to take the liberty of putting a question or two to you."

"All right, grannie. Fire away."

"Will you tell me, then, what the object of this world is?"

"Well, most people makes it their object to get money, and make theirselves comfortable."

"But you don't think that is what the world was made for?"

"Oh! as to that, how should I know, grannie? And not knowin', I won't say."

"If you saw a scaffold," said Marion, turning again to Jarvis, "would you be in danger of mistaking it for a permanent erection?"

"Nobody wouldn't be such a fool," he answered. "The look of it would tell you that."

"You wouldn't complain, then, if it should be a little out of the square, and if there should be no windows in it?"

Jarvis only laughed.

"Mr. Evans," Marion went on, turning again to the blind man, "do you think the design of this world was to make men comfortable?"

"If it was, it don't seem to ha' succeeded," answered Evans.

"And you complain of that—don't you?"

"Well, yes, rather,"—said the blind man, adding, no doubt, as he recalled the former part of the evening's talk,—"for harguyment, ye know, grannie."

"You think, perhaps, that God, having gone so far to make this world a pleasant and comfortable place to live in, might have gone farther and made it quite pleasant and comfortable for everybody?"

"Whoever could make it at all could ha' done that, grannie."

"Then, as he hasn't done it, the probability is he didn't mean to do it?"

"Of course. That's what I complain of."

"Then he meant to do something else?"

"It looks like it."

"The whole affair has an unfinished look, you think?"

"I just do."

"What if it were not meant to stand, then? What if it were meant only for a temporary assistance in carrying out something finished and lasting, and of unspeakably more importance? Suppose God were building a palace for you, and had set up a scaffold, upon which he wanted you to help him; would it be reasonable in you to complain that you didn't find the scaffold at all a comfortable place to live in?—that it was draughty and cold? This World is that scaffold; and if you were busy carrying stones and mortar for the palace, you would be glad of all the cold to cool the glow of your labor."

"I'm sure I work hard enough when I get a job as my heyesight will enable me to do," said Evans, missing the spirit of her figure.

"Yes: I believe you do. But what will all the labor of a workman who does not fall in with the design of the builder come to? You may say you don't understand the design: will you say also that you are under no obligation to put so much faith in the builder, who is said to be your God and Father, as to do the thing he tells you? Instead of working away at the palace, like men, will you go on tacking bits of matting and old carpet about the corners of the scaffold to keep the wind off, while that same wind keeps tearing them away and scattering them? You keep trying to live in a scaffold, which not all you could do to all eternity would make a house of. You see what I mean, Mr. Evans?"

"Well, not ezackly," replied the blind man.

"I mean that God wants to build you a house whereof the walls shall be *goodness*: you want a house whereof the walls shall be *comfort*. But God knows that such walls cannot be built,—that that kind of stone crumbles away in the foolish workman's hands. He would make you comfortable; but neither is that his first object, nor can it be gained without the first, which is to make you good. He loves you so much that he would infinitely rather have you good and uncomfortable, for then he could take you to his heart as his own children, than comfortable and not good, for then he could not come near you, or give you any thing he counted worth having for himself or worth giving to you."

"So," said Jarvis, "you've just brought us round, grannie, to the same thing as before."

"I believe so," returned Marion. "It comes to this, that when God would build a palace for himself to dwell in with his children, he does not want his scaffold so constructed that they shall be able to make a house of it for themselves, and live like apes instead of angels."

"But if God can do any thing he please," said Evans, "he might as well *make* us good, and there would be an end of it."

"That is just what he is doing," returned Marion. "Perhaps, by giving them perfect health, and every thing they wanted, with absolute good temper, and making them very fond of each other besides, God might have provided himself a people he would have had no difficulty in governing, and amongst whom, in consequence, there would have been no crime and no struggle or suffering. But I have known a dog with more goodness than that would come to. We cannot be good without having consented to be made good. God shows us the good and the bad; urges us to be good; wakes good thoughts and desires in us; helps our spirit with his Spirit, our thought with his thought: but we must yield; we must turn to him; we must consent, yes, try to be made good. If we could grow good without trying, it would be a poor goodness: *we* should not be good, after all; at best, we should only be not bad. God wants us to choose to be good, and so be partakers of his holiness; he would have us lay hold of him. He who has given his Son to suffer for us will make us suffer too, bitterly if needful, that we may bethink ourselves, and turn to him. He would make us as good as good can be, that is, perfectly good; and therefore will rouse us to take the needful hand in the work ourselves,—rouse us by discomforts innumerable.

"You see, then, it is not inconsistent with the apparent imperfections of the creation around us, that Jesus should have done the best possible carpenter's work; for those very imperfections are actually through their imperfection the means of carrying out the higher creation God has in view, and at which he is working all the time.

"Now let me read you what King David thought upon this question."

She read the hundred and seventh Psalm. Then they had some singing, in which the children took a delightful part. [pp. 256-274]

❖ Chapter 4 ❖
THOMAS WINGFOLD, CURATE

A Church of England curate, Thomas Wingfold appears in three MacDonald novels. He is the main character in *Thomas Wingfold, Curate*, one of the major characters in *Paul Fabor, Surgeon,* and a minor character in *There and Back*. When we first meet him he is a young curate who is challenged by an atheist about his beliefs. The atheist, Bascombe, asks him if he actually believes what he is preaching and for the first time in his life, he must really think about it. Thomas has drifted into the ministry as a safe profession and he must admit that he doesn't know what he does believe. His sermons have been taken from an uncle's sermons and are not really his own. At about the same time, Joseph Polworth informs him that his latest sermon is straight from Jeremy Taylor. It seems that Wingfold's uncle had plagiarized his sermons as well. Polworth is one of MacDonald's ideal Christians and becomes a mentor for Thomas. Thomas wants to seek for the truth but doesn't know what to do. He believes that he should resign. However, Polworth advises him to continue while he is seeking. His advice is "to let them [the parishioners] know that you wished it understood between them and you that you did not profess to teach them anything of yourself, but merely to bring to bear upon them the teaching of others." This is the plan he adopts and the following sermons show his journey to faith.

"A Strange Sermon"

"'Confess your faults one to another.'—This command of the apostle, my hearers, ought to justify me in doing what I fear some of you may consider almost as a breach of morals—talking of myself in the pulpit. But in the pulpit has a wrong been done, and in the pulpit shall it be confessed. From Sunday to Sunday, standing on this spot, I have read to you, without word of explanation, as if they formed the message I had sought and found for you, the thoughts and words of another. Doubtless they were better than any I could have given you from my own mind or experience, and the act had been a righteous one, had I told you the truth concerning them. But that truth I did not tell you.—At last, through words of honest expostulation, the voice of a friend whose wounds are faithful, I have been aroused to a knowledge of the wrong I have been doing. Therefore I now confess it. I am sorry. I will do so no more.

"But, brethren, I have only a little garden on a bare hill-side, and it hath never yet borne me any fruit fit to offer for your acceptance; also, my heart is troubled about many things, and God hath humbled me. I beg of you, therefore, to bear with me for a little while, if, doing what is but lawful and expedient both, I break through the bonds of custom in order to provide you with food convenient for you. Should I fail in this, I shall make room for a better man. But for your bread of this day, I go gleaning openly in other men's fields—fields into which I could not have found my way, in time at least for your necessities, and where I could not have gathered such full ears of wheat, barley, and oats but for the more than assistance of the same friend who warned me of the wrong I was doing both you and myself. Right ancient fields are some of them, where yet the ears lie thick for the gleaner. To continue my metaphor: I will lay each handful before you with the name of the field where I gathered it; and together they will serve to show what some of the wisest and best shepherds of the English flock have believed concerning the duty of confessing our faults."

He then proceeded to read the extracts which Mr. Polwarth had helped him to find—and arrange, not chronologically, but after an idea of growth. Each handful, as he called it, he prefaced with one or two words concerning him in whose field he had gleaned it.

His voice steadied and strengthened as he read. Renewed contact with the minds of those vanished teachers gave him a delight which infused itself into the uttered words, and made them also joyful; and if the curate preached to no one else in the congregation, certainly he preached to himself, and before it was done had entered into a thorough enjoyment of the sermon.

A few in the congregation were disappointed because they had looked for a justification and enforcement of the confessional, thinking the change in the curate could only have come from that portion of the ecclesiastical heavens towards which they themselves turned their faces. A few others were scandalized at such an innovation on the part of a young man who was only a curate. Many however declared that it was the most interesting sermon they had ever heard in their lives—which perhaps was not saying much. [pp. 94-96]

"THE CURATE MAKES A DISCOVERY"

"WHY CALL YE ME LORD, LORD, AND DO NOT THE THINGS WHICH I SAY?"

"My hearers, I come before you this morning to utter the first word of truth it has ever been given to ME to utter."

His hearers stared both mentally and corporeally.

"Is he going to deny the Bible?" said some.

—"It will be the last," said others, "if the rector hear in time how you have been disgracing yourself and profaning his pulpit."

"And," the curate went on, "it would be as a fire in my bones did I attempt to keep it back.

"In my room, three days ago, I was reading the strange story of the man who appeared in Palestine saying that he was the Son of God, and came upon those words of his which I have now read in your hearing. At their sound the accuser, Conscience, awoke in my bosom, and asked, 'Doest thou the things he saith to thee?' And I thought with myself,— 'Have I this day done anything he says to me?—when did I do anything I had heard of him? Did I ever'—to this it came at last—'Did I ever, in all my life, do one thing because he said to me DO THIS?' And the answer was NO, NEVER. Yet there I was, not only calling myself a Christian, but on the strength of my Christianity, it was to be presumed, living amongst you, and received by you, as your helper on the way to the heavenly kingdom—a living falsehood, walking and talking amongst you!"

"What a wretch!" said one man to himself, who made a large part of his living by the sale of under-garments whose every stitch was an untacking of the body from the soul of a seamstress. "Bah!" said some. "A hypocrite, by his own confession!" said others. "Exceedingly improper!" said Mrs. Ramshorn. "Unheard-of and most unclerical behaviour! And actually to confess such paganism!" For Helen, she waked up a little, began to listen, and wondered what he had been saying that a wind seemed to have blown rustling among the heads of the congregation.

"Having made this confession," Wingfold proceeded, "you will understand that whatever I now say, I say to and of myself as much as to and of any other to whom it may apply."

He then proceeded to show that faith and obedience are one and the same spirit, passing as it were from room to room in the same heart: what in the heart we call faith, in the will we call obedience. He showed that the Lord refused absolutely the faith that found its vent at the lips in the worshipping words, and not at the limbs in obedient action—which some present pronounced bad theology, while others said to themselves surely that at least was common sense.

He closed at length with these words:

"After the confession I have now made to you, a confession which I have also entreated everyone to whom it belongs to make to himself and his God, it follows that I dare not call myself a Christian. How should such a one as I know anything about that which, if it be true at all, is the loftiest, the one all-absorbing truth in the universe? How should such a fellow as I"—he went on, growing scornful at himself in the presence of the truth—"judge of its sacred probabilities? or, having led such a life of simony, be heard when he declares that such a pretended message from God to men seems too good to be true? The things therein contained I declare good, yet went not and did them. Therefore am I altogether out of court, and must not be heard in the matter.

"No, my hearers, I call not myself a Christian, but I call everyone here who obeys the word of Jesus, who restrains anger, who declines judgment, who practises generosity, who loves his enemies, who prays for his slanderers, to witness my vow, that I will henceforth try to obey him, in the hope that he whom he called God and his Father, will reveal to him whom you call your Lord Jesus Christ, that into my darkness I may receive the light of the world!"

"A professed infidel!" said Mrs. Ramshorn. "A clever one too! That was a fine trap he laid for us, to prove us all atheists as well as himself! As if any mere mortal COULD obey the instructions of the Saviour! He was divine; we are but human!" [pp. 150-154]

"Another Sermon"

His first sermon is enough to show that he had begun to have thoughts of his own—a very different thing from the entertaining of the thoughts of others, however well we may feed and lodge them—thoughts which came to him not as things which sought an entrance, but as things that sought an exit—cried for forms of embodiment that they might pass out of the infinite, and by incarnation become communicable.

The news of that strange first sermon had of course spread through the town, and the people came to church the next Sunday in crowds— twice as many as the usual assembly—some who went seldom, some who went nowhere, some who belonged to other congregations and communities—mostly bent on witnessing whatever eccentricity the very peculiar young man might be guilty of next, but having a few among them who were sympathetically interested in seeing how far his call, if call it was, would lead him.

His second sermon was to the same purport as the first. Preposing no text, he spoke to the following effect, and indeed the following are of the very words he uttered:

"The church wherein you now listen, my hearers, the pulpit wherein I now speak, stand here from of old in the name of Christianity. What is Christianity? I know but one definition, the analysis of which, if the thing in question be a truth, must be the joyous labour of every devout heart to all eternity. For Christianity does not mean what you think or what I think concerning Christ, but what IS OF Christ. My Christianity, if ever I come to have any, will be what of Christ is in me; your Christianity now is what of Christ is in you. Last Sunday I showed you our Lord's very words—that he, and no other, was his disciple who did what he told him,—and said therefore that I dared not call myself a disciple. I say the same thing in saying now that I dare not call myself a Christian, lest I should offend him with my 'Lord, Lord!' Still it is, and I cannot now help it, in the name of Christianity that I here stand. I have, alas, with blameful and appalling thoughtlessness I subscribed my name, as a believer, to the Articles of the Church of England, with no better reason than that I was unaware of any dissent therefrom, and have been ordained one of her ministers. The relations into which this has brought me I do not feel justified in severing at once, lest I should therein seem to deny that which its own illumination may yet show me to be true, and I desire therefore a little respite and room for thought and resolve. But meantime it remains my business, as an honest man in the employment of the church, to do my best towards the setting forth of the claims of him upon whom that church is founded, and in whose name she exists. As one standing on the outskirts of a listening Galilean crowd, a word comes now and then to my hungry ears and hungrier heart: I turn and tell it again to you—not that ye have not heard it also, but that I may stir you up to ask yourselves: 'Do I then obey this word? Have I ever, have I once sought to obey it? Am I a pupil of Jesus? Am I a Christian?' Hear then of his words. For me, they fill my heart with doubt and dismay.

"The Lord says: Love your enemies. Sayest thou, It is impossible? Then dost thou mock the word of him who said, I am the Truth, and has no part in him. Sayest thou, Alas, I cannot? Thou sayest true, I doubt not. But hast thou tried whether he who made will not increase the strength put forth to obey him?

"The Lord says: Be ye perfect. Dost thou then aim after perfection, or dost thou excuse thy wilful short-comings, and say, To err is human—nor hopest that it may also be found human to grow divine? Then ask thyself, for thou hast good cause, whether thou hast any part in him.

"The Lord said, Lay not up for yourselves treasures on earth. My part is not now to preach against the love of money, but to ask you: Are you laying up for yourselves treasures on earth? As to what the command means, the honest heart and the dishonest must each settle in his own way; but if your heart condemn you, what I have to say is, Call not yourselves Christians, but consider whether you ought not to become disciples indeed. No doubt you can instance this, that, and the other man who does as you do, and of whom yet no man dreams of questioning the Christianity: it matters not a hair; all that goes but to say that you are pagans together. Do not mistake me: I judge you not. I but ask you, as mouthpiece most unworthy of that Christianity in the name of which this building stands and we are met therein, to judge your own selves by the words of its founder.

"The Lord said: Take no thought for your life. Take no thought for the morrow. Explain it as you may or can—but ask yourselves—Do I take no thought for my life? Do I take no thought for the morrow? and answer to yourselves whether or no ye are Christians.

"The Lord says: Judge not. Didst thou judge thy neighbour yesterday? Wilt thou judge him again to-morrow? Art thou judging him now in the very heart that within thy bosom sits hearing the words Judge not? Or wilt thou ask yet again—Who is my neighbour? How then canst thou look to be of those that shall enter through the gates into the city? I tell thee not, for I profess not yet to know anything, but doth not thy own profession of Christianity counsel thee to fall upon thy face, and cry to him whom thou mockest, 'I am a sinful man, O Lord'?

"The Lord said: All things whatsoever ye would that men should do to you, do ye even so to them. Ye that buy and sell, do you obey this law? Examine yourselves and see. Ye would that men should deal fairly by you; do you deal fairly by them as ye would count fairness in them to you?—If conscience makes you hang the head inwardly, however you sit with it erect in the pew, dare you add to your crime against the law and the prophets the insult to Christ of calling yourselves his disciples?

"Not every one that saith unto me, Lord, Lord, shall enter into the kingdom of heaven, but he that doeth the will of my Father which is in heaven. He will none but those who with him do the will of the Father." [pp. 178-181]

"A Sermon to Helen"

As usual his voice trembled at first, but rose into strength as his earnestness found way. This is a good deal like what he said:

"The marvellous man who is reported to have appeared in Palestine, teaching and preaching, seems to have suffered far more from sympathy with the inward sorrows of his race than from pity for their bodily pains. These last, could he not have swept from the earth with a word? and yet it seems to have been mostly, if not indeed always, only in answer to prayer that he healed them, and that for the sake of some deeper, some spiritual healing that should go with the bodily cure. It could not be for the dead man whom he was about to call from the tomb, that his tears flowed. What source could they have but compassion and pitiful sympathy for the sorrows of the dead man's sisters and friends who had not the inward joy that sustained himself, and the thought of all the pains and heartaches of those that looked in the face of death—the meanings of love—torn generations, the blackness of bereavement that had stormed through the ever changing world of human hearts since first man had been made in the image of his Father? Yet are there far more terrible troubles than this death—which I trust can only part, not keep apart. There is the weight of conscious wrong being and wrong doing—that is the gravestone that needs to be rolled away ere a man can rise to life. Call to mind how Jesus used to forgive men's sins, thus lifting from their hearts the crushing load that paralyzed all their efforts. Recall the tenderness with which he received those from whom the religious of his day turned aside—the repentant women who wept sore-hearted from very love, the publicans who knew they were despised because they were despicable. With him they sought and found shelter. He was their saviour from the storm of human judgment and the biting frost of public opinion, even when that opinion and that judgment were re-echoed by the justice of their own hearts. He received them, and the life within them rose up, and the light shone—the conscious light of light, despite even of shame and self-reproach. If God be for us who can be against us? In his name they rose from the hell of their own hearts' condemnation, and went forth to do the truth in strength and hope. They heard and believed and obeyed his words. And of all words that ever were spoken, were ever words gentler, tenderer, humbler, lovelier—if true, or more arrogant, man-degrading, God-defying—if false, than these, concerning which, as his, I now desire to speak to you: 'Come unto me, all ye that labour and are heavy-laden, and I will give you rest. Take my yoke upon you, and learn of me; for I am meek and lowly in heart: and ye shall find rest unto your souls. For my yoke is easy, and my burden is light'?

"Surely these words, could they but be heartily believed, are such as every human heart might gladly hear! What man is there who has not had, has not now, or will not have to class himself amongst the weary and heavy-laden? Ye who call yourselves Christians profess to believe such rest is to be had, yet how many of you go bowed to the very earth, and take no single step towards him who says Come, lift not an eye to see whether a face of mercy may not be looking down upon you! Is it that, after all, you do not believe there ever was such a man as they call Jesus? That can hardly be. There are few so ignorant, or so wilfully illogical as to be able to disbelieve in the existence of the man, or that he spoke words to this effect. Is it then that you are doubtful concerning the whole import of his appearance? In that case, were it but as a doubtful medicine, would it not be well to make some trial of the offer made? If the man said the words, he must have at least believed that he could fulfil them. Who that knows anything of him at all can for a moment hold that this man spoke what he did not believe? The best of the Jews who yet do not believe in him, say of him that he was a good though mistaken man. Will a man lie for the privilege of being despised and rejected of men, a man of sorrows and acquainted with grief? What but the confidence of truth could have sustained him when he knew that even those who loved him would have left him had they believed what he told them of his coming fate?—But then: believing what he said, might he not have been mistaken?—A man can hardly be mistaken as to whether he is at peace or not—whether he has rest in his soul or not. Neither I think can a man well be mistaken as to whence comes the peace he possesses,—as to the well whence he draws his comfort. The miser knows his comfort is his gold. Was Jesus likely to be mistaken when he supposed himself to know that his comfort came from his God? Anyhow he believed that his peace came from his obedience—from his oneness with the will of his Father. Friends, if I had such peace as was plainly his, should I not know well whence it came?—But I think I hear some one say: 'Doubtless the good man derived comfort from the thought of his Father, but might he not be mistaken in supposing there was any Father?' Hear me, my friends: I dare not say I know there is a Father. I dare not even say I think, I can only say with my whole heart I hope we have indeed a Father in heaven; but this man says HE KNOWS. Am I to say he does not know? Can I, who know so much I would gladly have otherwise in myself, imagine him less honest than I am? If he tells me he knows, I am dumb and listen. One I KNOW: THERE IS—outweighs a whole creation of voices crying each I KNOW NOT, THEREFORE THERE IS NOT. And observe it is his own, his own best he wants to give them—no bribe to obedience to his will, but the assurance of bliss if they will do as he does. He wants them to have peace— HIS peace—peace from the same source whence he has it. For what does he mean by TAKE MY YOKE UPON YOU, AND LEARN OF ME? He does not mean WEAR THE YOKE I LAY UPON YOU, AND OBEY MY WORDS. I do not say he might not have said so, or that he does not say what comes to the same thing at other times, but that is not what he says here—that is not the truth he would convey in these words. He means TAKE UPON YOU THE YOKE I WEAR; LEARN TO DO AS I DO, WHO SUBMIT EVERYTHING AND REFER EVERYTHING TO THE WILL OF MY FATHER, YEA HAVE MY WILL ONLY IN THE CARRYING OUT OF HIS: BE MEEK AND LOWLY IN HEART, AND YE SHALL FIND REST UNTO YOUR SOULS. With all the grief of humanity in his heart, in the face of the death that awaited him, he yet says, FOR MY YOKE, THE YOKE I WEAR, IS EASY, THE BURDEN I BEAR IS LIGHT. What made that yoke easy,—that burden light? That it was the will of the Father. If a man answer: 'Any good man who believed in a God, might say as much, and I do not see how it can help me;' my reply is, that this man says, COME UNTO ME, AND I WILL GIVE YOU REST—asserting the power to give perfect help to him that comes.—Does all this look far away, my friends, and very unlike the things about us? The things about you do not give you peace; from something different you may hope to gain it. And do not our souls themselves fall out with their surroundings, and cry for a nobler, better, more beautiful life?

"But some one will perhaps say: 'It is well; but were I meek and lowly in heart as he of whom you speak, it could not touch MY trouble: that springs not from myself, but from one I love.' I answer, if the peace be the peace of the Son of man, it must reach to every cause of unrest. And if thou hadst it, would it not then be next door to thy friend? How shall he whom thou lovest receive it the most readily—but through thee who lovest him? What if thy faith should be the next step to his? Anyhow, if this peace be not an all-reaching as well as a heart-filling peace; if it be not a righteous and a lovely peace, and that in despite of all surrounding and opposing troubles, then it is not the peace of God, for that passeth all understanding:—so at least say they who profess to know, and I desire to take them at their word. If thy trouble be a trouble thy God cannot set right, then either thy God is not the true God, or there is no true God, and the man who professed to reveal him led the one perfect life in virtue of his faith in a falsehood. Alas for poor men and women and their aching hearts!—If it offend any of you that I speak of Jesus as THE MAN who professed to reveal God, I answer, that the man I see, and he draws me as with the strength of the adorable Truth; but if in him I should certainly find the God for the lack of whose peace I and my brethren and sisters pine, then were heaven itself too narrow to hold my exultation, for in God himself alone could my joy find room.

"Come then, sore heart, and see whether his heart cannot heal thine. He knows what sighs and tears are, and if he knew no sin in himself, the more pitiful must it have been to him to behold the sighs and tears that guilt wrung from the tortured hearts of his brethren and sisters. Brothers, sisters, we MUST get rid of this misery of ours. It is slaying us. It is turning the fair earth into a hell, and our hearts into its fuel. There stands the man, who says he knows: take him at his word. Go to him who says in the might of his eternal tenderness and his human pity— COME UNTO ME, ALL YE THAT LABOUR AND ARE HEAVY-LADEN, AND I WILL GIVE YOU REST. TAKE MY YOKE UPON YOU, AND LEARN OF ME; FOR I AM MEEK AND LOWLY IN HEART: AND YE SHALL FIND REST UNTO YOUR SOULS. FOR MY YOKE IS EASY AND MY BURDEN IS LIGHT." [pp. 230-234]

"A Sermon to Leopold"

Leopold had committed a horrible crime and had trouble believing that he could be forgiven. Wingfold wanted to convince him, as well as others, that forgiveness and healing is always possible.

...and by the time he came to the sermon, thought of nothing but human hearts, their agonies, and him who came to call them to him.

"I came not to call the righteous, but sinners to repentance."

"Was it then of the sinners first our Lord thought ere he came from the bosom of the Father? Did the perfect will embrace in the all-atoning tenderness of the divine heart, the degraded, disfigured, defiled, distorted thing, whose angel is too blind ever to see the face of its Father? Through all the hideous filth of the charnel-house, which the passions had heaped upon her, did the Word recognise the bound, wing-lamed, feather-draggled Psyche, panting in horriblest torture? Did he have a desire to the work of his hands, the child of his father's heart, and therefore, strong in compassion, speed to the painful rescue of hearts like his own? That purity arid defilement should thus meet across all the great dividing gulf of law and morals! The friend of publicans and sinners! Think: he was absolutely friendly with them! was not shocked at them! held up no hands of dismay! Only they must do so no more.

"If he were to come again, visibly, now, which do you think would come crowding around him in greater numbers—the respectable church-goers, or the people from the slums? I do not know. I dare not judge. But the fact that the church draws so few of those that are despised, of those whom Jesus drew and to whom most expressly he came, gives ground for question as to how far the church is like her Lord. Certainly many a one would find the way to the feet of the master, from whom the respectable church-goer, the pharisee of our time, and the priest who stands on his profession, would draw back with disgust. And doubtless it would be in the religious world that a man like Jesus, who, without a professional education, a craftsman by birth and early training, uttered scarce a phrase endorsed by clerical use, or a word of the religious cant of the day, but taught in simplest natural forms the eternal facts of faith and hope and love, would meet with the chief and perhaps the only BITTER opponents of his doctrine and life.

"But did our Lord not call the righteous? Did he not call honest men about him—James and John and Simon—sturdy fisher-folk, who faced the night and the storm, worked hard, fared roughly, lived honestly, and led good cleanly lives with father and mother, or with wife and children? I do not know that he said anything special to convince them that they were sinners before he called them. But it is to be remarked that one of the first effects of his company upon Simon Peter was, that the fisherman grew ashamed of himself, and while ashamed was yet possessed with an impulse of openness and honesty no less than passionate. The pure man should not be deceived as to what sort of company he was in! 'Depart from me, for I am a sinful man, O Lord!' I would I could clearly behold with my mind's eye what he then saw in Jesus that drew from him that cry! He knew him for the Messiah: what was the working of the carpenter upon the fisherman that satisfied him of the fact? Would the miracle have done it but for the previous talk from the boat to the people? I think not. Anyhow St. Peter judged himself among the sinners, and we may be sure that if these fishers had been self-satisfied men, they would not have left all and gone after him who called them. Still it would hardly seem that it was specially as sinners that he did so. Again, did not men such as the Lord himself regarded as righteous come to him—Nicodemus, Nathaniel, the young man who came running and kneeled to him, the scribe who was not far from the kingdom, the centurion, in whom he found more faith than in any Jew, he who had built a synagogue in Capernaum, and sculptured on its lintel the pot of manna? These came to him, and we know he was ready to receive them. But he knew such would always come drawn of the Father; they did not want much calling; they were not so much in his thoughts therefore; he was not troubled about them; they were as the ninety and nine, the elder son at home, the money in the purse. Doubtless they had much to learn, were not yet in the kingdom, but they were crowding about its door. If I set it forth aright, I know not, but thus it looks to me. And one thing I cannot forget—it meets me in the face—that some at least,—who knows if not all?—of the purest of men have counted themselves the greatest sinners! Neither can I forget that other saying of our Lord, a stumbling-block to many—our Lord was not so careful as perhaps some would have had him, lest men should stumble at the truth—The first shall be last and the last first. While our Lord spoke the words: 'The time cometh that whosoever killeth you will think that he doeth God service,' even then was Saul of Tarsus at the feet of Gamaliel, preparing to do God that service; but like one born out of due time, after all the rest he saw the Lord, and became the chief in labour and suffering. Thus the last became first. And I bethink me that the beloved disciple, who leaned on the bosom of the Lord, who was bolder to ask him than any—with the boldness of love, he whom the meek and lowly called a Son of Thunder, was the last of all to rejoin the master in the mansions of his Father. Last or first—if only we are with him! One thing is clear that in the order of the Lord's business, first came sinners.

"Who that reflects can fail to see this at least, that a crime brings a man face to face with the reality of things? He who knows himself a sinner—I do not mean as one of the race— the most self-righteous man will allow that as a man he is a sinner—he to whom, in the words of the communion service, the remembrance of his sins is grievous, and the burden of them intolerable, knows in himself that he is a lost man. He can no more hold up his head among his kind; he cannot look a woman or a child in the face; he cannot be left alone with the chaos of his thoughts, and the monsters it momently breeds. The joys of his childhood, the delights of existence, are gone from him. There dwells within him an ever present judgment and fiery indignation. Such a man will start at the sound of pardon and peace, even as the camel of the desert at the scent of water. Therefore surely is such a man nearer to the gate of the kingdom than he against whom the world has never wagged a tongue, who never sinned against a social custom even, and has as easy a conscience as the day he was born; but who knows so little of himself that, while he thinks he is good enough, he carries within him the capacity and possibility of every cardinal sin, waiting only the special and fitting temptation which, like the match to the charged mine, shall set all in a roar! Of this danger he knows nothing, never dreams of praying against it, takes his seat in his pew Sunday after Sunday with his family, nor ever murmurs 'Lead us not into temptation' with the least sense that temptation is a frightful thing, but repeats and responds and listens in perfect self-satisfaction, doubting never that a world made up of such as he must be a pleasant sight in the eyes of the Perfect. There are men who will never see what they are capable or in danger of until they have committed some fearful wrong. Nay there are some for whom even that is not enough; they must be found out by their fellow-men, and scorned in the eyes of the world, before they can or will admit or comprehend their own disgrace. And there are worse still than these.

"But a man may be oppressed by his sins, and hardly know what it is that oppresses him. There is more of sin in our burdens than we are ourselves aware. It needs not that we should have committed any grievous fault. Do we recognize in ourselves that which needs to be set right, that of which we ought to be ashamed, something which, were we lifted above all worldly anxieties, would yet keep us uneasy, dissatisfied, take the essential gladness out of the sunlight, make the fair face of the earth indifferent to us, a trustful glance a discomposing look, and death a darkness?—I say to the man who feels thus, whatever he may have done or left undone, he is not so far from the kingdom of heaven but that he may enter thereinto if he will.

"And if there be here any soul withered up with dismay, torn with horrible wonder that he should have done the deed which he yet hath done, to him I say—Flee from the self that hath sinned and hide thee with Christ in God. Or if the words sound to thee as the words of some unknown tongue, and I am to thee as one that beateth the air, I say instead—Call aloud in thy agony, that, if there be a God, he may hear the voice of his child, and put forth his hand and lay hold upon him, and rend from him the garment that clings and poisons and burns, squeeze the black drop from his heart, and set him weeping like a summer rain. O blessed, holy, lovely repentance to which the Son of Man, the very root and man of men, hath come to call us! Good it is, and I know it. Come and repent with me, O heart wounded by thine own injustice and wrong, and together we will seek the merciful. Think not about thy sin so as to make it either less or greater in thine own eyes. Bring it to Jesus, and let him show thee how vile a thing it is. And leave it to him to judge thee—sure that he will judge thee justly, extenuating nothing, for he hath to cleanse thee utterly, and yet forgetting no smallest excuse that may cover the amazement of thy guilt, or witness for thee that not with open eyes didst thou do the deed. At the last he cried, 'Father forgive them, for they know not what they do.' For his enemies the truth should be spoken, his first words when they had nailed him to the cross. But again I say, let it be Christ that excuseth thee; he will do it to more purpose than thou, and will not wrong thy soul by excusing thee a hair too much, or thy heart by excusing thee a hair too little.

"I dreamed once that I had committed a terrible crime. Carried beyond myself by passion, I knew not at the moment HOW evil was the thing I did. But I knew it was evil. And suddenly I became aware, when it was too late, of the nature of that which I had done. The horror that came with the knowledge was of the things that belong only to the secret soul. I was the same man as before I did it, yet was I now a man of whom my former self could not have conceived the possibility as dwelling within it. The former self seemed now by contrast lovely in purity, yet out of that seeming purity this fearful, foul *I* of the present had just been born! The face of my fellow-man was an avenging law, the face of a just enemy. Where, how, should the frightful face be hidden? The conscious earth must take it into its wounded bosom, and that before the all-seeing daylight should come.

But it would come, and I should stand therein pointed at by every ray that shot through the sunny atmosphere!

"The agony was of its own kind, and I have no word to tell what it was like. An evil odour and a sickening pain combined, might be a symbol of the torture. As is in the nature of dreams, possibly I lay but a little second on the rack, yet an age seemed shot through and through with the burning meshes of that crime, while, cowering and terror-stricken, I tossed about the loathsome fact in my mind. I had DONE it, and from the done there was no escape: it was for evermore a thing done.— Came a sudden change: I awoke. The sun stained with glory the curtains of my room, and the light of light darted keen as an arrow into my very soul. Glory to God! I was innocent! The stone was rolled from my sepulchre. With the darkness whence it had sprung, the cloud of my crime went heaving lurid away. I was a creature of the light and not of the dark. For me the sun shone and the wind blew; for me the sea roared and the flowers sent up their odours. For me the earth had nothing to hide. My guilt was wiped away; there was no red worm gnawing at my heart; I could look my neighbour in the face, and the child of my friend might lay his hand in mine and not be defiled! All day long the joy of that deliverance kept surging on in my soul.

"But something yet more precious, more lovely than such an awaking, will repentance be to the sinner; for after all it was but a dream of the night from which that set me free, and the spectre-deed that vanished had never had a place in the world of fact; while the horror from which repentance delivers, is no dream, but a stubborn abiding reality. Again, the vanishing vision leaves the man what he was before, still capable it may be of committing the crime from which he is not altogether clean to whom in his sleep it was possible: repentance makes of the man a new creature, one who has awaked from the sleep of sin to sleep that sleep no more. The change in the one case is not for greatness comparable with that in the other. The sun that awakes from the one sleep, is but the outward sun of our earthly life—a glorious indeed and lovely thing, which yet even now is gathering a crust of darkness, blotting itself out and vanishing: the sun that awakes a man from the sleep of death is the living

Sun that casts from his thought out into being that other sun, with the space wherein it holds planetary court—the Father of lights, before whose shining in the inner world of truth eternal, even the deeds of vice become as spectral dreams, and, with the night of godlessness that engendered them, flee away.

"But a man may answer and say to me—'Thou art but borne on the wings of thine imagination. The fact of the crime remains, let a man tear out his heart in repentance, and no awaking can restore an innocence which is indeed lost.' I answer: The words thou speakest are in themselves true, yet thy ignorance makes them false. Thou knowest not the power of God, nor what resurrection from the dead means. What if, while it restored not thy former innocence, it brought thee a purity by the side of whose white splendour and inward preciousness, the innocence thou hadst lost was but a bauble, being but a thing that turned to dross in the first furnace of its temptation? Innocence is indeed priceless—that innocence which God counteth innocence, but thine was a flimsy show, a bit of polished and cherished glass—instead of which, if thou repentest, thou shalt in thy jewel-box find a diamond. Is thy purity, O fair Psyche of the social world, upon whose wings no spattering shower has yet cast an earthy stain, and who knowest not yet whether there be any such thing as repentance or need of the same!—is thy purity to compare with the purity of that heavenly Psyche, twice born, who even now in the twilight-slumbers of heaven, dreams that she washes with her tears the feet of her Lord, and wipes them with the hairs of her head? O bountiful God, who wilt give us back even our innocence tenfold! He can give an awaking that leaves the past of the soul ten times farther behind than ever waking from sleep left the dreams of the night.

"If the potency of that awaking lay in the inrush of a new billow of life, fresh from its original source, carrying with it an enlargement of the whole nature and its every part, a glorification of every faculty, every sense even, so that the man, forgetting nothing of his past or its shame, should yet cry out in the joy of his second birth: 'Lo! I am a new man; I am no more he who did that awful and evil thing, for I am no more capable of doing it! God be praised, for all is well!'—would not such an awaking send the past afar into the dim distance of the first creation, and wrap the ill deed in the clean linen cloth of forgiveness, even as the dull creature of the sea rolls up the grain of intruding sand in the lovely garment of a pearl? Such an awaking means God himself in the soul, not disdaining closest vital company with the creature he foresaw and created. And the man knows in full content that he is healed of his plague. Nor would he willingly lose the scars which record its outbreak, for they tell him what he is without God, and set him ever looking to see that the door into the heavenly garden stands wide for God to enter the house when it pleases him. And who can tell whether, in the train of such an awaking, may not follow a thousand opportunities and means of making amends to those whom he has injured?

"Nor must I fail to remind the man who has committed no grievous crime, that except he has repented of his evil self, and abjured all wrong, he is not safe from any, even the worst offence. There was a time when I could not understand that he who loved not his brother was a murderer: now I see it to be no figure of speech, but, in the realities of man's moral and spiritual nature, an absolute simple fact. The murderer and the unloving sit on the same bench before the judge of eternal truth. The man who loves not his brother, I do not say is at this moment capable of killing him, but if the natural working of his unlove be not checked, he will assuredly become capable of killing him. Until we love our brother, yes, until we love our enemy, who is yet our brother, we contain within ourselves the undeveloped germ of murder. And so with every sin in the tables or out of the tables. There is not one in this congregation who has a right to cast a look of reproach at the worst felon who ever sat in the prisoners' dock. I speak no hyperbole, but simple truth. We are very ready to draw in our minds a distinction between respectable sins—human imperfections we call them, perhaps—and disreputable vices, such as theft and murder; but there is no such distinction in fact. Many a thief is a better man than many a clergyman, and miles nearer to the gate of the kingdom. The heavenly order goes upon other principles than ours, and there are first that shall be last, and last that shall be first. Only, at the root of all human bliss lies repentance.

"Come then at the call of the Water, the Healer, the Giver of repentance and light, the Friend of publicans and sinners, all ye on whom lies the weight of a sin, or the gathered heap of a thousand crimes. He came to call such as you, that he might make you clear and clean. He cannot bear that you should live on in such misery, such badness, such blackness of darkness. He would give you again your life, the bliss of your being. He will not speak to you one word of reproach, except indeed you should aim at justifying yourselves by accusing your neighbour. He will leave it to those who cherish the same sins in their hearts to cast stones at you: he who has no sin casts no stone. Heartily he loves you, heartily he hates the evil in you—so heartily that he will even cast you into the fire to burn you clean. By making you clean he will give you rest. If he upbraid, it will not be for past sin, but for the present little faith, holding out to him an acorn-cup to fill. The rest of you keep aloof, if you will, until you shall have done some deed that compels you to cry out for deliverance; but you that know yourselves sinners, come to him that he may work in you his perfect work, for he came not to call the righteous, but sinners, us, you and me, to repentance." [pp. 333-342]

"THE CURATE'S RESOLVE"

And now this Sunday, Wingfold entered the pulpit prepared at last to utter his resolve. Happily nothing had been done to introduce the confusing element of another will. The bishop had heard nothing of the matter, and if anything had reached the rector, he had not spoken. Not one of the congregation, not even Mrs. Ramshorn, had hinted to him that he ought to resign. It had been left altogether with himself. And now he would tell them the decision to which the thought he had taken had conducted him. I will give a portion of his sermon—enough to show us how he showed the congregation the state of his mind in reference to the grand question, and the position he took in relation to his hearers.

"It is time, my hearers," he said, "because it is now possible, to bring to a close that uncertainty with regard to the continuance of our relation to each other, which I was, in the spring-time of the year, compelled by mental circumstance to occasion. I then forced myself, for very dread of the honesty of an all-knowing

God, to break through every convention of the church and the pulpit, and speak to you of my most private affairs. I told you that I was sure of not one of those things concerning which it is taken for granted that a clergyman must be satisfied; but that I would not at once yield my office, lest in that act I should seem to declare unbelief of many a thing which even then I desired to find true. In leaving me undisturbed either by complaint, expostulation, or proffered instruction, you, my hearers, have granted me the leisure of which I stood in need. Meantime I have endeavoured to show you the best I saw, while yet I dared not say I was sure of anything. I have thus kept you, those at least who cared to follow my path, acquainted with my mental history. And now I come to tell you the practical result at which I have arrived.

"But when I say that I will not forsake my curacy, still less my right and duty to teach whatever I seem to know, I must not therein convey the impression that I have attained that conviction and assurance the discovery of the absence of which was the cause of the whole uncertain proceeding. All I now say is, that in the story of Jesus I have beheld such grandeur—to me apparently altogether beyond the reach of human invention, such a radiation of divine loveliness and truth, such hope for man, soaring miles above every possible pitfall of Fate; and have at the same time, from the endeavour to obey the word recorded as his, experienced such a conscious enlargement of mental faculty, such a deepening of moral strength, such an enhancement of ideal, such an increase of faith, hope, and charity towards all men, that I now declare with the consent of my whole man—I cast in my lot with the servants of the Crucified; I am content even to share their delusion, if delusion it be, for it is the truth of the God of men to me; I will stand or fall with the story of my Lord; I will take my chance—I speak not in irreverence but in honesty—my chance of failure or success in regard to whatever may follow in this life or the life to come, if there be a life to come—on the words and will of the Lord Jesus Christ, whom if, impressed as I am with the truth of his nature, the absolute devotion of his life, and the essential might of his being, I yet obey not, I shall not only deserve to perish, but in that very refusal draw ruin upon my head. Before God I say it—I would rather be crucified with that man, so it might be as a disciple and not as a thief that creeps, intrudes, or climbs into the fold, than I would reign with him over such a kingdom of grandeur as would have satisfied the imagination and love-ambition of his mother. On such grounds as these I hope I am justified in declaring myself a disciple of the Son of Man, and in devoting my life and the renewed energy and enlarged, yea infinite hope which he has given me, to his brothers and sisters of my race, that if possible I may gain some to be partakers of the blessedness of my hope. Henceforth I am, not IN HOLY ORDERS, I reject the phrase, but UNDER holy orders, even the orders of Christ Jesus, which is the law of liberty, the law whose obedience alone can set a man free from in-burrowing slavery.

"And if any man yet say that, because of my lack of absolute assurance, I have no right to the sacred post,—Let him, I answer, who has been assailed by such doubts as mine, and from the citadel of his faith sees no more one lingering shadow of a foe—let him cast at me the first stone! Vain challenge! for such a one will never cast a stone at man or woman. But let not him whose belief is but the absence of doubt, who has never loved enough that which he thinks he believes to have felt a single fear lest it should not be true—let not that man, I say, cast at me pebble from the brook, or cloven rock from the mount of the law, for either will fall hurtless at my feet. Friends, I have for the last time spoken of myself in this place. Ye have borne with me in my trials, and I thank you. Those who have not only borne but suffered, and do now rejoice with me, I thank tenfold. I have done—

"Save for one word to the Christians of this congregation:

"The waves of infidelity are coming in with a strong wind and a flowing tide. Who is to blame? God it cannot be, and for unbelievers, they are as they were. It is the Christians who are to blame. I do not mean those who are called Christians, but those who call and count themselves Christians. I tell you, and I speak to each one of whom it is true, that you hold and present such a withered, starved, miserable, death's-head idea of Christianity; that you are yourselves such poverty-stricken believers, if believers you are at all; that the notion you present to the world as your ideal, is so commonplace, so false to the grand, gracious, mighty-hearted Jesus—that YOU are the cause why the truth hangs its head in patience, and rides not forth on the white horse, conquering and to conquer. You dull its lustre in the eyes of men; you deform its fair proportions; you represent not that which it is, but that which it is not, yet call yourselves by its name; you are not the salt of the earth, but a salt that has lost its savour, for ye seek all things else first, and to that seeking the kingdom of God and his righteousness shall never be added. Until you repent and believe afresh, believe in a nobler Christ, namely the Christ revealed by himself, and not the muffled form of something vaguely human and certainly not all divine, which the false interpretations of men have substituted for him, you will be, as, I repeat, you are, the main reason why faith is so scanty in the earth, and the enemy comes in like a flood. For the sake of the progress of the truth, and that into nobler minds than yours, it were better you joined the ranks of the enemy, and declared what I fear with many of you is the fact, that you believe not at all. But whether in some sense you believe or not, the fact remains, that, while you are not of those Christians who obey the word of the master, DOING the things he says to them, you are of those Christians, if you WILL be called by the name, to whom he will say, I never knew you: go forth into the outer darkness. Then at least will the church be rid of you, and the honest doubter will have room to breathe the divine air of the presence of Jesus.

"But oh what unspeakable bliss of heart and soul and mind and sense remains for him who like St. Paul is crucified with Christ, who lives no more from his own self, but is inspired and informed and possessed with the same faith towards the Father in which Jesus lived and wrought the will of the Father! If the words attributed to Jesus are indeed the words of him whom Jesus declared himself, then truly is the fate of mankind a glorious one,—and that, first and last, because men have a God supremely grand, all-perfect in God-head; for that is, and that alone can be, the absolute bliss of the created." [pp. 496-499]

❖ Chapter 5 ❖
PAUL FABER, SURGEON

Paul Faber, Surgeon contains three more sermons by Wingfold. The first is a sermon on God and Mammon, another version of the theme of a sermon in *Annals of a Quiet Neighbourhood*, recorded earlier.

"THE PULPIT"

"'Ye can not serve God and mammon.'

"Who said this? The Lord by whose name ye are called, in whose name this house was built, and who will at last judge every one of us. And yet how many of you are, and have been for years, trying your very hardest to do the thing your Master tells you is impossible! Thou man! Thou woman! I appeal to thine own conscience whether thou art not striving to serve God and mammon.

"But stay! am I right?—It can not be. For surely if a man strove hard to serve God and mammon, he would presently discover the thing was impossible. It is not easy to serve God, and it is easy to serve mammon; if one strove to serve God, the hard thing, along with serving mammon, the easy thing, the incompatibility of the two endeavors must appear. The fact is there is no strife in you. With ease you serve mammon every day and hour of your lives, and for God, you do not even ask yourselves the question whether you are serving Him or no. Yet some of you are at this very moment indignant that I call you servers of mammon. Those of you who know that God knows you are His servants, know also that I do not mean you; therefore, those who are indignant at being called the servants of mammon, are so because they are indeed such. As I say these words I do not lift my eyes, not that I am afraid to look you in the face, as uttering an offensive thing, but that I would have your own souls your accusers.

"Let us consider for a moment the God you do not serve, and then for a moment the mammon you do serve. The God you do not serve is the Father of Lights, the Source of love, the Maker of man and woman, the Head of the great family, the Father of fatherhood and motherhood; the Life-giver who would die to preserve His children, but would rather slay them than they should live the servants of evil; the God who can neither think nor do nor endure any thing mean or unfair; the God of poetry and music and every marvel; the God of the mountain tops, and the rivers that run from the snows of death, to make the earth joyous with life; the God of the valley and the wheat-field, the God who has set love betwixt youth and maiden; the God and Father of our Lord Jesus Christ, the perfect; the God whom Christ knew, with whom Christ was satisfied, of whom He declared that to know Him was eternal life. The mammon you do serve is not a mere negation, but a positive Death. His temple is a darkness, a black hollow, ever hungry, in the heart of man, who tumbles into it every thing that should make life noble and lovely. To all who serve him he makes it seem that his alone is the reasonable service. His wages are death, but he calls them life, and they believe him. I will tell you some of the marks of his service—a few of the badges of his household— for he has no visible temple; no man bends the knee to him; it is only his soul, his manhood, that the worshiper casts in the dust before him. If a man talks of the main chance, meaning thereby that of making money, or of number one, meaning thereby self, except indeed he honestly jest, he is a servant of mammon. If, when thou makest a bargain, thou thinkest only of thyself and thy gain, thou art a servant of mammon. The eager looks of those that would get money, the troubled looks of those who have lost it, worst of all the gloating looks of them that have it, these are sure signs of the service of mammon. If in the church thou sayest to the rich man, 'Sit here in a good place,' and to the poor man, 'Stand there,' thou art a mammon-server. If thou favorest the company of those whom men call well-to-do, when they are only well-to-eat, well-to-drink, or well-to-show, and declinest that of the simple and the meek, then in thy deepest consciousness know that thou servest mammon, not God. If thy hope of well-being in time to come, rests upon thy houses, or lands, or business, or money in store, and not upon the living God, be thou friendly and kind with the overflowings of thy possessions, or a churl whom no man loves, thou art equally a server of mammon. If the loss of thy goods would take from thee the joy of thy life; if it would tear thy heart that the men thou hadst feasted should hold forth to thee the two fingers instead of the whole hand; nay, if thy thought of to-morrow makes thee quail before the duty of to-day, if thou broodest over the evil that is not come, and turnest from the God who is with thee in the life of the hour, thou servest mammon; he holds thee in his chain; thou art his ape, whom he leads about the world for the mockery of his fellow-devils. If with thy word, yea, even with thy judgment, thou confessest that God is the only good, yet livest as if He had sent thee into the world to make thyself rich before thou die; if it will add one feeblest pang to the pains of thy death, to think that thou must leave thy fair house, thy ancestral trees, thy horses, thy shop, thy books, behind thee, then art thou a servant of mammon, and far truer to thy master than he will prove to thee. Ah, slave! the moment the breath is out of the body, lo, he has already deserted thee! and of all in which thou didst rejoice, all that gave thee such power over thy fellows, there is not left so much as a spike of thistle-down for the wind to waft from thy sight. For all thou hast had, there is nothing to show. Where is the friendship in which thou mightst have invested thy money, in place of burying it in the maw of mammon? Troops of the dead might now be coming to greet thee with love and service, hadst thou made thee friends with thy money; but, alas! to thee it was not money, but mammon, for thou didst love it—not for the righteousness and salvation thou by its means mightst work in the earth, but for the honor it brought thee among men, for the pleasures and immunities it purchased. Some of you are saying in your hearts, 'Preach to thyself, and practice thine own preaching;'—and you say well. And so I mean to do, lest having preached to others I should be myself a cast-away—drowned with some of you in the same pond of filth. God has put money in my power through the gift of one whom you know. I shall endeavor to be a faithful steward of that which God through her has committed to me in trust. Hear me, friends—to none of you am I the less a friend that I tell you truths you would hide from your own souls: money is not mammon; it is God's invention; it is good and the gift of God. But for money and the need of it, there would not be half the friendship in the world. It is powerful for good when divinely used. Give it plenty of air, and it is sweet as the hawthorn; shut it up, and it cankers and breeds worms. Like all the best gifts of God, like the air and the water, it must have motion and change and shakings asunder; like the earth itself, like the heart and mind of man, it must be broken and turned, not heaped together and neglected. It is an angel of mercy, whose wings are full of balm and dews and refreshings; but when you lay hold of him, pluck his pinions, pen him in a yard, and fall down and worship him—then, with the blessed vengeance of his master, he deals plague and confusion and terror, to stay the idolatry. If I misuse or waste or hoard the divine thing, I pray my Master to see to it - my God to punish me. Any fire rather than be given over to the mean idol! And now I will make an offer to my townsfolk in the face of this congregation—that, whoever will, at the end of three years, bring me his books, to him also will I lay open mine, that he will see how I have sought to make friends of the mammon of unrighteousness. Of the mammon-server I expect to be judged according to the light that is in him, and that light I know to be darkness.

"Friend, be not a slave. Be wary. Look not on the gold when it is yellow in thy purse. Hoard not. In God's name, spend—spend on. Take heed how thou spendest, but take heed that thou spend. Be thou as the sun in heaven; let thy gold be thy rays, thy angels of love and life and deliverance. Be thou a candle of the Lord to spread His light through the world. If hitherto, in any fashion of faithlessness, thou hast radiated darkness into the universe, humble thyself, and arise and shine.

"But if thou art poor, then look not on thy purse when it is empty. He who desires more than God wills him to have, is also a servant of mammon, for he trusts in what God has made, and not in God Himself. He who laments what God has taken from him, he is a servant of mammon. He who for care can not pray, is a servant of mammon. There are men in this town who love and trust their horses more than the God that made them and their horses too. None the less confidently will they give judgment on the doctrine of God. But the opinion of no man who does not render back his soul to the living God and live in Him, is, in religion, worth the splinter of a straw. Friends, cast your idol into the furnace; melt your mammon down, coin him up, make God's money of him, and send him coursing. Make of him cups to carry the gift of God, the water of life, through the world—in lovely justice to the oppressed, in healthful labor to them whom no man hath hired, in rest to the weary who have borne the burden and heat of the day, in joy to the heavy-hearted, in laughter to the dull-spirited. Let them all be glad with reason, and merry without revel. Ah! what gifts in music, in drama, in the tale, in the picture, in the spectacle, in books and models, in flowers and friendly feasting, what true gifts might not the mammon of unrighteousness, changed back into the money of God, give to men and women, bone of our bone, and flesh of our flesh! How would you not spend your money for the Lord, if He needed it at your hand! He does need it; for he that spends it upon the least of his fellows, spends it upon his Lord. To hold fast upon God with one hand, and open wide the other to your neighbor—that is religion; that is the law and the prophets, and the true way to all better things that are yet to come.—Lord, defend us from Mammon. Hold Thy temple against his foul invasion. Purify our money with Thy air, and Thy sun, that it may be our slave, and Thou our Master. Amen." [pp. 30-35]

"The Groans of the Inarticulate"

This sermon was given after a surgeon's helper had performed vivisection on a dog.

As the curate went up the pulpit-stair, he felt as if the pulse of all creation were beating in unison with his own; for to-day he was the speaker for the speechless, the interpreter of groans to the creation of God.

He read, Are not two sparrows sold for a farthing? and one of them shall not fall on the ground without your Father: and said:

"My friends, doth God care for sparrows? Or saith He it altogether for our sakes, and not at all for the sparrows? No, truly; for indeed it would be nothing to us if it were not every thing to the sparrows. The word can not reach our door except through the sparrow's nest. For see! what comfort would it be to us to be told we were of more value than ever so many sparrows, if their value was nothing—if God only knew and did not care for them? The saying would but import that we were of more value than just nothing. Oh, how skillful is unbelief to take all the color and all the sweetness and all the power out of the words of The Word Himself! How many Christians are there not who take the passage to mean that not a sparrow can fall to the ground without the knowledge of its Creator! A mighty thing that for the sparrow! If such a Christian seemed to the sparrow the lawful interpreter of the sparrow's Creator, he would make an infidel of the sparrow. What Christ-like heart, what heart of loving man, could be content to take all the comfort to itself, and leave none for the sparrows? Not that of our mighty brother Paul. In his ears sounded, in his heart echoed, the cries of all the creation of God. Their groanings that could not be uttered, roused the response of his great compassion. When Christ was born in the heart of Paul, the whole creation of God was born with him; nothing that could feel could he help loving; in the trouble of the creatures' troubles, sprang to life in his heart the hope, that all that could groan should yet rejoice, that on the lowest servant in the house should yet descend the fringe of the robe that was cast about the redeemed body of the Son. He was no pettifogging priest standing up for the rights of the superior! An exclusive is a self-excluded Christian. They that shut the door will find themselves on the wrong side of the door they have shut. They that push with the horn and stamp with the hoof, can not be admitted to the fold. St. Paul would acknowledge no distinctions. He saw every wall—of seclusion, of exclusion, of partition, broken down. Jew and Greek, barbarian, Scythian, bond and free—all must come in to his heart. Mankind was not enough to fill that divine space, enlarged to infinitude by the presence of the Christ: angels, principalities, and powers, must share in its conscious splendor. Not yet filled, yet unsatisfied with beings to love, Paul spread forth his arms to the whole groaning and troubled race of animals. Whatever could send forth a sigh of discomfort, or heave a helpless limb in pain, he took to the bosom of his hope and affection—yea, of his love and faith: on them, too, he saw the cup of Christ's heart overflow. For Paul had heard, if not from His own, yet from the lips of them that heard Him speak, the words, **Are not five sparrows sold for two farthings, and not one of them is forgotten before God?** What if the little half-farthing things bear their share, and always have borne, in that which is behind of the sufferings of Christ? In any case, not one of them, not one so young that it topples from the edge of its nest, unable to fly, is forgotten by the Father of men. It shall not have a lonely deathbed, for the Father of Jesus will be with it. It must be true. It is indeed a daring word, but less would not be enough for the hearts of men, for the glory of God, for the need of the sparrow. I do not close my eyes to one of a thousand seemingly contradictory facts. I misdoubt my reading of the small-print notes, and appeal to the text, yea, beyond the text, even to the God of the sparrows Himself.

"I count it as belonging to the smallness of our faith, to the poorness of our religion, to the rudimentary condition of our nature, that our sympathy with God's creatures is so small. Whatever the narrowness of our poverty-stricken, threadbare theories concerning them, whatever the inhospitality and exclusiveness of our mean pride toward them, we can not escape admitting that to them pain is pain, and comfort is comfort; that they hunger and thirst; that sleep restores and death delivers them: surely these are ground enough to the true heart wherefore it should love and cherish them—the heart at least that believes with St. Paul, that they need and have the salvation of Christ as well as we. Right grievously, though blindly, do they groan after it.

"The ignorance and pride which is forever sinking us toward them, are the very elements in us which mislead us in our judgment concerning them, causing us to imagine them not upon a lower merely, but upon an altogether different footing in creation from our own. The same things we call by one name in us, and by another in them. How jealous have not men been as to allowing them any share worthy the name of reason! But you may see a greater difference in this respect between the lowest and the highest at a common school, than you will between them and us. A pony that has taught itself without hands to pump water for its thirst, an elephant that puts forth its mighty lip to lift the moving wheel of the heavy wagon over the body of its fallen driver, has rather more to plead on the score of intellect than many a schoolboy. Not a few of them shed tears. A bishop, one of the foremost of our scholars, assured me that once he saw a certain animal laugh while playing off a practical joke on another of a different kind from himself. I do not mention the kind of animal, because it would give occasion for a silly articulate joke, far inferior to his practical one. I go further, and say, that I more than suspect a rudimentary conscience in every animal. I care not how remotely rudimentary. There must be in the moral world absolute and right potent germinal facts which lie infinitudes beyond the reach of any moral microscope, as in the natural world beyond the most powerful of lenses. Yet surely in this respect also, one may see betwixt boys at the same school greater differences than there are betwixt the highest of the animals and the lowest of the humans. If you plead for time for the boy to develop his poor rudimentary mollusk of a conscience, take it and heartily welcome—but grant it the animals also. With some of them it may need millions of years for any thing I know. Certainly in many human beings it never comes plainly into our ken all the time they walk the earth. Who shall say how far the vision of the apostle reached? but surely the hope in which he says God Himself subjected the creature to vanity, must have been an infinite hope: I will hope infinitely. That the Bible gives any ground for the general fancy that at death an animal ceases to exist, is but the merest dullest assumption. Neither is there a single scientific argument, so far as I know, against the continued existence of the animals, which would not tell equally against human immortality. My hope is, that in some way, concerning which I do not now choose to speculate, there may be progress, growth, for them also. While I believe for myself, I **must** hope for them. This much at least seems clear—and I could press the argument further: if not one of them is forgotten before God—and one of them yet passes out of being—then is God the God of the dead and not of the living! But we praise Thee, we bless Thee, we worship Thee, we glorify Thee, we give thanks to Thee for Thy great glory, O Lord God, heavenly King, God the Father almighty! Thy universe is life, life and not death. Even the death which awoke in the bosom of Sin, Thy Son, opposing Himself to its hate, and letting it spend its fury upon Him, hath abolished. I know nothing, therefore care little, as to whether or not it may have pleased God to bring man up to the hill of humanity through the swamps and thickets of lower animal nature, but I do care that I should not now any more approach that level, whether once rightly my own or not. For what is honor in the animals, would be dishonor in me. Not the less may such be the punishment, perhaps redemption, in store for some men and women. For aught I know, or see unworthy in the thought, the self-sufficing exquisite, for instance, may one day find himself chattering amongst fellow apes in some monkey-village of Africa or Burmah. Nor is the supposition absurd, though at first sight it may well so appear. Let us remember that we carry in us the characteristics of each and every animal. There is not one fiercest passion, one movement of affection, one trait of animal economy, one quality either for praise or blame, existing in them that does not exist in us. The relationship can not be so very distant. And if theirs be so freely in us, why deny them so much we call ours? Hear how one of the ablest doctors of the English church, John Donne, Dean of St. Paul's in the reign of James the first, writes:—

> Man is a lump where all beasts kneaded be;
> Wisdom makes him an ark where all agree;
> The fool, in whom these beasts do live at jar,
> Is sport to others, and a theater;
> Nor scapes he so, but is himself their prey;
> All which was man in him, is eat away;
> And now his beasts on one another feed,
> Yet couple in anger, and new monsters breed.
> How happy's he which hath due place assigned
> To his beasts, and disaforested his mind!
> Impaled himself to keep them out, not in;
> Can sow, and dares trust corn where they have been;
> Can use his horse, goat, wolf, and every beast,

And is not ass himself to all the rest!
Else man not only is the herd of swine,
But he's those devils, too, which did incline
Them to an headlong rage, and made them worse;
For man can add weight to heaven's heaviest curse.

"It astonishes me, friends, that we are not more terrified at ourselves. Except the living Father have brought order, harmony, a world, out of His chaos, a man is but a cage of unclean beasts, with no one to rule them, however fine a gentleman he may think himself. Even in this fair, well-ordered England of ours, at Kirkdale, in Yorkshire, was discovered, some fifty years ago, a great cavern that had once been a nest of gigantic hyenas, evidenced by their own broken bones, and the crushed bones of tigers, elephants, bears, and many other creatures. See to what a lovely peace the Creating Hand has even now brought our England, far as she is yet from being a province in the kingdom of Heaven; but see also in her former condition a type of the horror to which our souls may festering sink, if we shut out His free spirit, and have it no more moving upon the face of our waters. And when I say a type, let us be assured there is no type worth the name which is not poor to express the glory or the horror it represents.

"To return to the animals: they are a care to God! they occupy part of His thoughts; we have duties toward them, owe them friendliness, tenderness. That God should see us use them as we do is a terrible fact—a severe difficulty to faith. For to such a pass has the worship of Knowledge—an idol vile even as Mammon himself, and more cruel—arrived, that its priests, men kind as other men to their own children, kind to the animals of their household, kind even to some of the wild animals, men who will scatter crumbs to the robins in winter, and set water for the sparrows on their house-top in summer, will yet, in the worship of this their idol, in their greed after the hidden things of the life of the flesh, without scruple, confessedly without compunction, will, I say, dead to the natural motions of the divine element in them, the inherited pity of God, subject innocent, helpless, appealing, dumb souls to such tortures whose bare description would justly set me forth to the blame of cruelty toward those who sat listening to the same. Have these living, moving, seeing, hearing, feeling creatures, who could not be but by the will and the presence of Another any more than ourselves—have they no rights in this their compelled existence? Does the most earnest worship of an idol excuse robbery with violence extreme to obtain the sacrifices he loves? Does the value of the thing that may be found there justify me in breaking into the house of another's life? Does his ignorance of the existence of that which I seek alter the case? Can it be right to water the tree of knowledge with blood, and stir its boughs with the gusts of bitter agony, that we may force its flowers into blossom before their time? Sweetly human must be the delights of knowledge so gained! grand in themselves, and ennobling in their tendencies! Will it justify the same as a noble, a laudable, a worshipful endeavor to cover it with the reason or pretext—God knows which—of such love for my own human kind as strengthens me to the most ruthless torture of their poorer relations, whose little treasure I would tear from them that it may teach me how to add to their wealth? May my God give me grace to prefer a hundred deaths to a life gained by the suffering of one simplest creature. He holds his life as I hold mine by finding himself there where I find myself. Shall I quiet my heart with the throbs of another heart? soothe my nerves with the agonized tension of a system? live a few days longer by a century of shrieking deaths? It were a hellish wrong, a selfish, hateful, violent injustice. An evil life it were that I gained or held by such foul means! How could I even attempt to justify the injury, save on the plea that I am already better and more valuable than he; that I am the stronger; that the possession of all the pleasures of human intelligence gives me the right to turn the poor innocent joys of his senses into pains before which, threatening my own person, my very soul would grow gray with fear? Or let me grant what many professional men deny utterly, that some knowledge of what is called practical value to the race has been thus attained—what can be its results at best but the adding of a cubit to the life? Grant that it gave us an immortal earthly existence, one so happy that the most sensual would never wish for death: what would it be by such means to live forever? God in Heaven! who, what is the man who would dare live a life wrung from the agonies of tortured innocents? Against the will of my Maker, live by means that are an abhorrence to His soul! Such a life must be all in the flesh! the spirit could have little share therein. Could it be even a life of the flesh that came of treason committed against essential animality? It could be but an abnormal monstrous existence, that sprang, toadstool-like, from the blood-marsh of cruelty— a life neither spiritual nor fleshey, but devilish.

"It is true we are above the creatures—but not to keep them down; they are for our use and service, but neither to be trodden under the foot of pride, nor misused as ministers, at their worst cost of suffering, to our inordinate desires of ease. After no such fashion did God give them to be our helpers in living. To be tortured that we might gather ease! none but a devil could have made them for that! When I see a man who professes to believe not only in a God, but such a God as holds His court in the person of Jesus Christ, assail with miserable cruelty the scanty, lovely, timorous lives of the helpless about him, it sets my soul aflame with such indignant wrath, with such a sense of horrible incongruity and wrong to every harmony of Nature, human and divine, that I have to make haste and rush to the feet of the Master, lest I should scorn and hate where He has told me to love. Such a wretch, not content that Christ should have died to save men, will tear Christ's living things into palpitating shreds, that he may discover from them how better to save the same men. Is this to be in the world as He was in the world! Picture to yourselves one of these Christian inquirers erect before his class of students: knife in hand, he is demonstrating to them from the live animal, so fixed and screwed and wired that he cannot find for his agony even the poor relief of a yelp, how this or that writhing nerve or twitching muscle operates in the business of a life which his demonstration has turned from the gift of love into a poisoned curse; picture to yourself such a one so busied, suddenly raising his eyes and seeing the eyes that see him! the eyes of Him who, when He hung upon the cross, knew that He suffered for the whole creation of His Father, to lift it out of darkness into light, out of wallowing chaos into order and peace! Those eyes watching him, that pierced hand soothing his victim, would not the knife fall from his hand in the divine paralysis that shoots from the heart and conscience? Ah me! to have those eyes upon me in any wrong-doing! One thing only could be worse - **not** to have them upon me—to be left with my devils.

"You all know the immediate cause of the turning of our thoughts in this direction—the sad case of cruelty that so unexpectedly rushed to light in Glaston. So shocked was the man in whose house it took place that, as he drove from his door the unhappy youth who was guilty of the crime, this testimony, in the righteous indignation of his soul, believing, as you are aware, in no God and Father of all, broke from him with curses—'There ought to be a God to punish such cruelty. Begone,' he said. 'Never would I commit woman or child into the hands of a willful author of suffering.'

"We are to rule over the animals; the opposite of rule is torture, the final culmination of anarchy. We slay them, and if with reason, then with right. Therein we do them no wrong. Yourselves will bear me witness however and always in this place, I have protested that death is no evil, save as the element of injustice may be mingled therein. The sting of death is sin. Death, righteously inflicted, I repeat, is the reverse of an injury.

"What if there is too much lavishment of human affection upon objects less than human! it hurts less than if there were none. I confess that it moves with strange discomfort one who has looked upon swarms of motherless children, to see in a childless house a ruined dog, overfed, and snarling with discomfort even on the blessed throne of childhood, the lap of a woman. But even that is better than that the woman should love no creature at all—infinitely better! It may be she loves as she can. Her heart may not yet be equal to the love of a child, may be able only to cherish a creature whose oppositions are merely amusing, and whose presence, as doubtless it seems to her, gives rise to no responsibilities. Let her love her dog—even although her foolish treatment of him should delay the poor animal in its slow trot towards canine perfection: she may come to love him better; she may herself through him advance to the love and the saving of a child—who can tell? But do not mistake me; there are women with hearts so divinely insatiable in loving, that in the mere gaps of their untiring ministration of humanity, they will fondle any living thing capable of receiving the overflow of their affection. Let such love as they will; they can hardly err. It is not of such that I have spoken.

"Again, to how many a lonely woman is not life made endurable, even pleasant, by the possession and the love of a devoted dog! The man who would focus the burning glass of science upon the animal, may well mock at such a mission, and speak words contemptuous of the yellow old maid with her yellow ribbons and her yellow dog. Nor would it change his countenance or soften his heart to be assured that that withered husk of womanhood was lovely once, and the heart in it is loving still; that she was reduced to all but misery by the self-indulgence of a brother, to whom the desolation of a sister was but a pebble to pave the way to his pleasures; that there is no one left her now to love, or to be grateful for her love, but the creature which he regards merely as a box of nature's secrets, worthy only of being rudely ransacked for what it may contain, and thrown aside when shattered in the search. A box he is indeed, in which lies inclosed a shining secret!—a truth too radiant for the eyes of such a man as he; the love of a living God is in him and his fellows, ranging the world in broken incarnation, ministering to forlorn humanity in dumb yet divine service. Who knows, in their great silence, how germane with ours may not be their share in the groanings that can not be uttered!

"Friends, there must be a hell. If we leave scripture and human belief aside, science reveals to us that nature has her catastrophes—that there is just so much of the failed cycle, of the unrecovered, the unbalanced, the incompleted, the fallen-short, in her motions, that the result must be collision, shattering resumption, the rage of unspeakable fire. Our world and all the worlds of the system, are, I suppose, doomed to fall back at length into their parent furnace. Then will come one end and another beginning. There is many an end and many a beginning. At one of those ends, and that not the furthest, must surely lie a hell, in which, of all sins, the sin of cruelty, under whatever pretext committed, will receive its meed from Him with whom there is no respect of persons, but who giveth to every man according to his works. Nor will it avail him to plead that in life he never believed in such retribution; for a cruelty that would have been restrained by a fear of hell was none the less hellworthy.

"But I will not follow this track. The general conviction of humanity will be found right against any conclusions calling themselves scientific, that go beyond the scope or the reach of science. Neither will I presume to suggest the operation of any lex talionis in respect of cruelty. I know little concerning the salvation by fire of which St. Paul writes in his first epistle to the Corinthians; but I say this, that if the difficulty of curing cruelty be commensurate with the horror of its nature, then verily for the cruel must the furnace of wrath be seven times heated. Ah! for them, poor injured ones, the wrong passes away! Friendly, lovely death, the midwife of Heaven, comes to their relief, and their pain sinks in precious peace. But what is to be done for our brother's soul, bespattered with the gore of innocence? Shall the cries and moans of the torture he inflicted haunt him like an evil smell? Shall the phantoms of exquisite and sickening pains float lambent about the fingers, and pass and repass through the heart and brain, that sent their realities quivering and burning into the souls of the speechless ones? It has been said somewhere that the hell for the cruel man would be to have the faces of all the creatures he had wronged come staring round him, with sad, weary eyes. But must not the divine nature, the pitiful heart of the universe, have already begun to reassert itself in him, before that would hurt him? Upon such a man the justice in my heart desires this retribution—to desire more would be to be more vile than he; to desire less would not be to love my brother:—that the soul capable of such deeds shall be compelled to know the nature of its deeds in the light of the absolute Truth—that the eternal fact shall flame out from the divine region of its own conscience until it writhe in the shame of being itself, loathe as absolute horror the deeds which it would now justify, and long for deliverance from that which it has made of itself. The moment the discipline begins to blossom, the moment the man begins to thirst after confession and reparation, then is he once more my brother; then from an object of disgust in spite of pity, he becomes a being for all tender, honest hearts in the universe of God to love, cherish, revere.

"Meantime, you who behold with aching hearts the wrongs done to the lower brethren that ought to be cherished as those to whom less has been given, having done all, stand comforted in the thought that not one of them suffers without the loving, caring, sustaining presence of the great Father of the universe, the Father of men, the God and Father of Jesus Christ, the God of the sparrows and the ravens and the oxen—yea, of the lilies of the field." [pp. 171-181]

"A Conscience"

"Beware ye of the leaven of the Pharisees, which is hypocrisy. For there is nothing covered, that shall not be revealed; neither hid, that shall not be known."

*Then at once he began to show them, in the simplest interpretation, that the hypocrite was one who pretended to be what he was not; who tried or consented to look other and better than he was. That a man, from unwillingness to look at the truth concerning himself, might be but half-consciously assenting to the false appearance, would, he said, nowise serve to save him from whatever of doom was involved in this utterance of our Lord concerning the crime. These words of explanation and caution premised, he began at the practical beginning, and spoke a few forceful things on the necessity of absolute truth as to fact in every communication between man and man, telling them that, so far as he could understand His words recorded, our Lord's objection to swearing lay chiefly in this, that it encouraged untruthfulness, tending to make a man's yea less than yea, his nay other than nay. He said that many people who told lies every day, would be shocked when they discovered that they were liars; and that their lying must be discovered, for the Lord said so. Every untruthfulness was a passing hypocrisy, and if they would not come to be hypocrites out and out, they must begin to avoid it by speaking every man the truth to his neighbor. If they did not begin at once to speak the truth, they must grow worse and worse liars. The Lord called hypocrisy **leaven**, because of its irresistible, perhaps as well its unseen, growth and spread; he called it the leaven **of the pharisees**, because it was the all-pervading quality of their being, and from them was working moral dissolution in the nation, eating like a canker into it, by infecting with like hypocrisy all who looked up to them.*

"Is it not a strange drift, this of men," *said the curate*, "to hide what is, under the veil of what is not? to seek refuge in lies, as if that which is not, could be an armor of adamant? to run from the daylight for safety, deeper into the cave? In the cave house the creatures of the night—the tigers and hyenas, the serpent and the old dragon of the dark; in the light are true men and women, and the clear-eyed angels. But the reason is only too plain; it is, alas! that they are themselves of the darkness and not of the light. They do not fear their own. They are more comfortable with the beasts of darkness than with the angels of light. They dread the peering of holy eyes into their hearts; they feel themselves naked and fear to be ashamed, therefore cast the garment of hypocrisy about them. They have that in them so strange to the light that they feel it must be hidden from the eye of day, as a thing *hideous*, that is, a thing to be hidden. But the hypocrisy is worse than all it would hide. That they have to hide again, as a more hideous thing still.

"God hides nothing. His very work from the beginning is *revelation*—a casting aside of veil after veil, a showing unto men of truth after truth. On and on, from fact to fact divine He advances, until at length in His Son Jesus, He unveils His very face. Then begins a fresh unveiling, for the very work of the Father is the work the Son Himself has to do—to reveal. His life was the unveiling of Himself, and the unveiling of the Son is still going on, and is that for the sake of which the world exists. When He is unveiled, that is, when we know the Son, we shall know the Father also. The whole of creation, its growth, its history, the gathering total of human existence, is an unveiling of the Father. He is the life, the eternal life, the *Only*. I see it—ah! believe me—I see it as I can not say it. From month to month it grows upon me. The lovely home-light, the One essence of peaceful being, is God Himself.

"He loves light and not darkness, therefore shines, therefore reveals. True, there are infinite gulfs in Him, into which our small vision can not pierce, but they are gulfs of light, and the truths there are invisible only through excess of their own clarity. There is a darkness that comes of effulgence, and the most veiling of all veils is the light. That for which the eye exists is light, but *through* light no human eye can pierce.—I find myself beyond my depth. I am ever beyond my depth, afloat in an infinite sea; but the depth of the sea knows me, for the ocean of my being is God.—What I would say is this, that the light is not blinding because God would hide, but because the truth is too glorious for our vision. The effulgence of Himself God veiled that He might unveil it—in his Son. Inter-universal spaces, aeons, eternities—what word of vastness you can find or choose—take unfathomable darkness itself, if you will, to express the infinitude of God, that original splendor existing only to the consciousness of God Himself—I say He hides it not, but is revealing it ever, forever, at all cost of labor, yea of pain to Himself. His whole creation is a sacrificing of Himself to the being and well-being of His little ones, that, being wrought out at last into partakers of His divine nature, that nature may be revealed in them to their divinest bliss. He brings hidden things out of the light of His own being into the light of ours.

"But see how different *we* are—until we learn of Him! See the tendency of man to conceal his treasures, to claim even truth as his own by discovery, to hide it and be proud of it, gloating over that which he thinks he has in himself, instead of groaning after the infinite of God! We would be forever heaping together possessions, dragging things into the cave of our finitude, our individual self, not perceiving that the things which pass that dreariest of doors, whatever they may have been, are thenceforth but 'straws, small sticks, and dust of the floor.' When a man would have a truth in thither as if it were of private interpretation, he drags in only the bag which the truth, remaining outside, has burst and left.

"Nowhere are such children of darkness born as in the caves of hypocrisy; nowhere else can a man revel with such misshapen hybrids of religion and sin. But, as one day will be found, I believe, a strength of physical light before which even solid gold or blackest marble becomes transparent, so is there a spiritual light before which all veils of falsehood shall shrivel up and perish and cease to hide; so that, in individual character, in the facts of being, in the densest of Pharisaical hypocrisy, there is nothing covered that shall not be revealed, nothing hid that shall not be known.

"If then, brother or sister, thou hast that which would be hidden, make haste and drag the thing from its covert into the presence of thy God, thy Light, thy Saviour, that, if it be in itself good, it may be cleansed; if evil, it may be stung through and through with the burning arrows of truth, and perish in glad relief. For the one bliss of an evil thing is to perish and pass; the evil thing, and that alone, is the natural food of Death—nothing else will agree with the monster. If we have such foul things, I say, within the circumference of our known selves, we must confess the charnel-fact to ourselves and to God; and if there be any one else who has a claim to know it, to that one also must we confess, casting out the vile thing that we may be clean. Let us make haste to open the doors of our lips and the windows of our humility, to let out the demon of darkness, and in the angels of light—so abjuring the evil. Be sure that concealment is utterly, absolutely hopeless. If we do not thus ourselves open our house, the day will come when a roaring blast of His wind, or the flame of His keen lightning, will destroy every defense of darkness, and set us shivering before the universe in our naked vileness; for there is nothing covered that shall not be revealed, neither hid that shall not be known. Ah! well for man that he can not hide! What vaults of uncleanness, what sinks of dreadful horrors, would not the souls of some of us grow! But for every one of them, as for the universe, comes the day of cleansing. Happy they who hasten it! who open wide the doors, take the broom in the hand, and begin to sweep! The dust may rise in clouds; the offense may be great; the sweeper may pant and choke, and weep, yea, grow faint and sick with self-disgust; but the end will be a clean house, and the light and wind of Heaven shining and blowing clear and fresh and sweet through all its chambers. Better so, than have a hurricane from God burst in doors and windows, and sweep from his temple with the besom of destruction every thing that loveth and maketh a lie. Brothers, sisters, let us be clean. The light and the air around us are God's vast purifying furnace; out into it let us cast all hypocrisy. Let us be open-hearted, and speak every man the truth to his neighbor. Amen." [pp. 215-218]

CHAPTER 6

THERE AND BACK

In this novel, Lady Wylder's favorite son has died and she blames God for it. Even though this child was her favorite, she still treated him cruelly at times. She manifests her hatred of God by lounging in her pew and reading a novel during Thomas Wingfold's sermons. Thomas does not know how he should handle this situation; she is not only annoying him but defying God and bothering the whole congregation. Finally Mrs. Wingfold suggests that her husband "preach at her." Although Wingfold does not like to do this, he finally decides to preach the following sermon. At the beginning of the sermon, Mrs. Wylder is again ostentatiously reading her novel in the face of the congregation. Her reaction to Wingfold's words is given at the end of the sermon. Later in the novel, Wingfold is able to help her overcome her hatred.

"THE PARSON'S PARABLE"

"My friends, I will follow the example of our Lord, and speak to you to-day in a parable. The Lord said there are things better spoken in parables, because of the eyes that will not see, and the ears that will not hear.

"There was once a mother left alone with her little boy—the only creature in the world or out of it that she cared for. She was a good mother to him, as good a mother as you can think, never overbearing or unkind. She never thought of herself, but always of the desire of her heart, the apple of her eye, her son born of her own body. It was not because of any return he could make her that she loved him. It was not to make him feel how good she was, that she did everything for him. It was not to give him reasons for loving *her*, but because she loved *him*, and because he needed her. He was a delicate child, requiring every care she could lavish upon him, and she did lavish it. Oh, how she loved him! She would sit with the child on her lap from morning till night, gazing on him; she always went to sleep with him in her bosom—as close to her as ever he could lie. When she woke in the dark night, her first movement was to strain him closer, her next to listen if he was breathing—for he might have died and been lost! When he looked up at her with eyes of satisfaction, she felt all her care repaid.

"The years went on, and the child grew, and the mother loved him more and more. But he did not love her as she loved him. He soon began to care for the things she gave him, but he did not learn to love the mother who gave them. Now the whole good of things is to be the messengers of love—to carry love from the one heart to the other heart; and when these messengers are fetched instead of sent, grasped at, that is, by a greedy, ungiving hand, they never reach the heart, but block up the path of love, and divide heart from heart; so that the greedy heart forgets the love of the giving heart more and more, and all by the things it gives. That is the way generosity fares with the ungenerous. The boy would be very pleasant to his mother so long as he thought to get something from her; but when he had got what he wanted, he would forget her until he wanted something more.

"There came at last a day when she said to him, 'Dear boy, I want you to go and fetch me some medicine, for I feel very poorly, and am afraid I am going to be ill!' He mounted his pony, and rode away to get the medicine. Now his mother had told him to be very careful, because the medicine was dangerous, and he must not open the bottle that held it. But when he had it, he said to himself, 'I dare say it is something very nice, and mother does not want me to have any of it!' So he opened the bottle and tasted what was in it, and it burned him terribly. Then he was furious with his mother, and said she had told him not to open the bottle just to make him do it, and vowed he would not go back to her! He threw the bottle from him, and turned, and rode another way, until he found himself alone in a wild forest, where was nothing to eat, and nothing to shelter him from the cold night, and the wind that blew through the trees, and made strange noises. He dismounted, afraid to ride in the dark, and before he knew, his pony was gone. Then he began to be miserably frightened, and to wish he had not run away. But still he blamed his mother, who might have known, he said, that he would open the bottle.

"The mother got very uneasy about her boy, and went out to look for him. The neighbours too, though he was not a nice boy, and none but his mother liked him, went out also, for they would gladly find him and take him home to her; and they came at last to the wood, with their torches and lanterns.

"The boy was lying under a tree, and saw the lights, and heard the voices, and knew it was his mother come. Then the old wickedness rose up fresh in his heart, and he said to himself: 'She shall have trouble yet before she finds me! Am I to come and go as she pleases!' He lay very still; and when he saw them coming near, crept farther, and again lay still. Thus he went on doing, and so avoided his saviours. He heard one say there were wolves in the wood, for that was the sound of them; but he was just the kind of boy that will not believe, but thinks every one has a purpose of his own in saying this or that. So he slipped and slipped away until at length all despaired of finding him, and left the wood.

"Suddenly he knew that he was again alone. He gave a great shriek, but no one heard it. He stood quaking and listening. Presently his pony came rushing past him, with two or three wolves behind him. He started to his feet and began to run, wild to get out of the wood. But he could not find the way, and ran about this way and that until utter despair came down upon him, and all he could do was to lie still as a mouse lest the wolves should hear him.

"And as he lay he began at last to think that he was a wicked child; that his mother had done everything to make him good, and he would not be good; and now he was lost, and the wolves alone would find him! He sank at last into a stupor, and lay motionless, with death and the wolves after him.

"He came to himself in the arms of a strange woman, who had taken him up, and was carrying him home.

"The name of the woman was Sorrow—a wandering woman, a kind of gypsy, always going about the world, and picking up lost things. Nobody likes her, hardly anybody is civil to her; but when she has set anybody down and is gone, there is often a look of affection and wonder and gratitude sent after her. For all that, however, very few are glad to be found by her again.

"Sorrow carried him weeping home to his mother. His mother came out, and took him in her arms. Sorrow made her courtesy, and went away. The boy clung to his mother's neck, and said he was sorry. In the midst of her joy his mother wept bitterly, for he had nearly broken her heart. She could not get the wolves out of her mind.

"But, alas! the boy forgot all, and was worse than ever. He grew more and more cruel to his mother, and mocked at every word she said to him; so that—"

There came a cry from the gallery. The congregation started in sudden terror to their feet. The rector stopped, and turning to the right, stood gazing. In the front of the squire's pew stood Mrs. Wylder, white, and speechless with rage. For a moment she stood shaking her fist at the preacher. Then, in a hoarse broken voice, came the words—

"It's a lie. My boy was never cruel to me. It's a wicked lie."

She could say no more, but stood and glared, hate in her fierce eyes, and torture in her colourless face.

"Madam, you have betrayed yourself," *said the rector solemnly.* "If your son behaved well to you, it makes it the worse in you to behave ill to your Father. From Sunday to Sunday you insult him with rude behaviour. I tell you so in the face of this congregation, which knows it as well as I. Hitherto I have held my tongue—from no fear of the rich, from no desire to spare them deserved disgrace in the eyes of the poor, but because I shrank from making the house of God a place of contention. Madam, you have behaved shamefully, and I do my duty in rebuking you."

The whole congregation were on their feet, staring at her. A moment she stood, and would have brazened out the stare. But she felt the eyes of the motionless hundreds blazing upon her, and the culprit soul grew naked in the presence of judging souls. Her nerve gave way; she turned her back, left the pew, and fled from the church by the squire's door, into the grounds of Wylder Hall. [pp. 115-118]

CHAPTER 7

ADELA CATHART

Adela Cathcart contains two sermons and can be shown without giving the context in the story. The first is a Christmas sermon.

"CHURCH"

"It is not the high summer alone that is God's. The winter also is His. And into His winter He came to visit us. And all man's winters are His—the winter of our poverty, the winter of our sorrow, the winter of our unhappiness—even 'the winter of our discontent.'

"Winter," *he went on*, "does not belong to death, although the outside of it looks like death. Beneath the snow, the grass is growing. Below the frost, the roots are warm and alive. Winter is only a spring too weak and feeble for us to see that it is living. The cold does for all things what the gardener has sometimes to do for valuable trees: he must half kill them before they will bear any fruit. Winter is in truth the small beginnings of the spring.

"The winter is the childhood of the year. Into this childhood of the year came the child Jesus; and into this childhood of the year must we all descend. It is as if God spoke to each of us according to our need: My son, my daughter, you are growing old and cunning; you must grow a child again, with my son, this blessed birth-time. You are growing old and selfish; you must become a child. You are growing old and careful; you must become a child. You are growing old and distrustful; you must become a child. You are growing old and petty, and weak, and foolish; you must become a child—my child, like the baby there, that strong sunrise of faith and hope and love, lying in his mother's arms in the stable.

"But one may say to me: 'You are talking in a dream. The Son of God is a child no longer. He is the King of Heaven.' True, my friends. But He who is the Unchangeable, could never become anything that He was not always, for that would be to change. He is as much a child now as ever he was. When he became a child, it was only to show us by itself, that we might understand it better, what he was always in his deepest nature. And when he was a child, he was not less the King of Heaven; for it is in virtue of his childhood, of his sonship, that he is Lord of Heaven and of Earth—'for of such'—namely, of children—'is the kingdom of heaven" And, therefore, when we think of the baby now, it is still of the Son of man, of the King of men, that we think. And all the feelings that the thought of that babe can wake in us, are as true now as they were on that first Christmas day, when Mary covered from the cold his little naked feet, ere long to be washed with the tears of repentant women, and nailed by the hands of thoughtless men, who knew not what they did, to the cross of fainting, and desolation, and death."

"So, my friends, let us be children this Christmas. Of course, when I say to anyone, 'You must be like a child,' I mean a good child. A naughty child is not a child as long as his naughtiness lasts. He is not what God meant when He said, 'I will make a child.' Think of the best child you know—the one who has filled you with most admiration. It is his child-likeness that has so delighted you. It is because he is so true to the child-nature that you admire him. Jesus is like that child. You must be like that child. But you cannot help knowing some faults in him—some things that are like ill-grown men and women. Jesus is not like him, there. Think of the best child you can imagine; nay, think of a better than you can imagine—of the one that God thinks of when he invents a child in the depth of his fatherhood: such child-like men and women must you one day become; and what day better to begin, than this blessed Christmas Morn? Let such a child be born in your hearts this day. Take the child Jesus to your bosoms, into your very souls, and let him grow there till he is one with your every thought, and purpose, and hope. As a good child born in a family will make the family good; so Jesus, born into the world, will make the world good at last. And this perfect child, born in your hearts, will make your hearts good; and that is God's best gift to you.

"Then be happy this Christmas Day; for to you a child is born. Childless women, this infant is yours—wives or maidens. Fathers and mothers, he is your first-born, and he will save his brethren. Eat and drink, and be merry and kind, for the love of God is the source of all joy and all good things, and this love is present in the child Jesus - Now, to God the Father, &c. [pp. 18-20]

"The Curate and his Wife"

"My friends, I will give you a likeness, or a parable, which I think will help you to understand what is the matter with you all. For you all have something the matter with you; and most of you know this to be the case; though you may not know what is the matter. And those of you that feel nothing amiss are far the worst off. Indeed you are; for how are things to be set right if you do not even know that there is anything to be set right? There is the greatest danger of everything growing much worse, before you find out that anything is wrong.

"But now for my parable.

"It is a cold winter forenoon, with the snow upon everything out of doors. The mother has gone out for the day, and the children are amusing themselves in the nursery—pretending to make such things as men make. But there is one among them who joins in their amusement only by fits and starts. He is pale and restless, yet inactive.—His mother is away. True, he is not well. But he is not very unwell; and if she were at home, he would take his share in everything that was going on, with as much enjoyment as any of them. But as it is, his fretfulness and pettishness make no allowance for the wilfulness of his brothers and sisters; and so the confusions they make in the room, carry confusion into his heart and brain; till at length a brighter noon entices the others out into the snow.

"Glad to be left alone, he seats himself by the fire and tries to read. But the book he was so delighted with yesterday, is dull to-day. He looks up at the clock and sighs, and wishes his mother would come home. Again he betakes himself to his book, and the story transports his imagination to the great icebergs on the polar sea. But the sunlight has left them, and they no longer gleam and glitter and sparkle, as if spangled with all the jewels of the hot tropics, but shine cold and threatening as they tower over the ice-bound ship. He lays down the tale, and takes up a poem. But it too is frozen. The rhythm will not flow. And the sad feeling arises in his heart, that it is not so very beautiful, after all, as he had used to think it.

"'Is there anything beautiful?' says the poor boy at length, and wanders to the window. But the sun is under a cloud; cold, white, and cheerless, like death, lies the wide world out of doors; and the prints of his mother's feet in the snow, all point towards the village, and away from home. His head aches; and he cannot eat his dinner. He creeps up stairs to his mother's room. There the fire burns bright, and through the window falls a ray of sunlight. But the fire and the very sunlight are wintry and sad. 'Oh, when will mother be home?' He lays himself in a corner amongst soft pillows, and rests his head; but it is no nest for him, for the covering wings are not there. The bright-coloured curtains look dull and grey; and the clock on the chimney-piece will not hasten its pace one second, but is very monotonous and unfeeling. Poor child! Is there any joy in the world? Oh yes; but it always clings to the mother, and follows her about like a radiance, and she has taken it with her. Oh, when will she be home? The clock strikes as if it meant something, and then straightway goes on again with the old wearisome tic-tac.

"He can hardly bear it. The fire burns up within, daylight goes down without; the near world fades into darkness; the far-off worlds brighten and come forth, and look from the cold sky into the warm room; and the boy stares at them from the couch, and watches the motion of one of them, like the flight of a great golden beetle, against the divisions of the window-frame. Of this, too, he grows weary. Everything around him has lost its interest. Even the fire, which is like the soul of the room, within whose depths he had so often watched for strange forms and images of beauty and terror, has ceased to attract his tired eyes. He turns his back to it, and sees only its flickerings on the walls. To any one else, looking in from the cold frosty night, the room would appear the very picture of afternoon comfort and warmth; and he, if he were descried thus nestling in its softest, warmest nook, would be counted a blessed child, without care, without fear, made for enjoyment, and knowing only fruition. But the mother is gone; and as that flame-lighted room would appear to the passing eye, without the fire, and with but a single candle to thaw the surrounding darkness and cold, so is that child's heart without the presence of the mother.

"Worn out at length with loneliness and mental want, he closes his eyes, and after the slow lapse of a few more empty moments, re-opens them on the dusky ceiling, and the grey twilight window; no—on two eyes near above him, and beaming upon him, the stars of a higher and holier heaven than that which still looks in through the unshaded windows. They are the eyes of the mother, looking closely and anxiously on her sick boy. 'Mother, mother!' His arms cling around her neck, and pull down her face to his.

"His head aches still, but the heart-ache is gone. When candles are brought, and the chill night is shut out of doors and windows, and the children are all gathered around the tea-table, laughing and happy, no one is happier, though he does not laugh, than the sick child, who lies on the couch and looks at his mother. Everything around is full of interest and use, glorified by the radiation of her presence. Nothing can go wrong. The splendour returns to the tale and the poem. Sickness cannot make him wretched. Now when he closes his eyes, his spirit dares to go forth wandering under the shining stars and above the sparkling snow; and nothing is any more dull and unbeautiful. When night draws on, and he is laid in his bed, her voice sings him, and her hand soothes him, to sleep; nor do her influences vanish when he forgets everything in sleep; for he wakes in the morning well and happy, made whole by his faith in his mother. A power has gone forth from her love to heal and restore him.

"Brothers sisters! do I not know your hearts from my own?—sick hearts, which nothing can restore to health and joy but the presence of Him who is Father and Mother both in one. Sunshine is not gladness, because you see him not. The stars are far away, because He is not near; and the flowers, the smiles of old Earth, do not make you smile, because, although, thank God! you cannot get rid of the child's need, you have forgotten what it is the need of. The winter is dreary and dull, because, although you have the homeliest of homes, the warmest of shelters, the safest of nests to creep into and rest—though the most cheerful of fires is blazing for you, and a table is spread, waiting to refresh your frozen and weary hearts—you have forgot the way thither, and will not be troubled to ask the way; you shiver with the cold and the hunger, rather than arise [and] say, 'I will go to my Father;' you will die in the storm rather than fight the storm; you will lie down in the snow rather than tread it under foot. The heart within you cries out for something, and you let it cry. It is crying for its God—for its father and mother and home. And all the world will look dull and grey—and it if does not look so now, the day will come when it must look so—till your heart is satisfied and quieted with the known presence of Him in whom we live and move and have our being." [pp. 181-185]

❖ CHAPTER 8 ❖
SALTED WITH FIRE

In this novel, James Baltherwick was a young preacher who committed a serious sin. He repented of it and resigned as a minister. A godly man, a shoemaker, helped James through his difficulties. This sermon is given in the dialect as in the book. If the reader has trouble understanding the dialect, there is a translation included at the end of the sermon.

When the soutar [shoemaker] began [to preach,] James was a little shocked at first to hear him use his mother-tongue as in his ordinary conversation; but any sense of its unsuitableness vanished presently, and James soon began to feel that the vernacular gave his friend additional power of expression, and therewith of persuasion.

"My frien's, I was jist thinkin, as I cam ower the hill," he began, "hoo we war a' made wi' differin pooers—some o' 's able to dee ae thing best, and some anither; and that led me to remark, that it was the same wi' the warl we live in—some pairts o' 't fit for growin aits, and some bere, and some wheat, or pitatas; and hoo ilk varyin rig had to be turnt til its ain best eese. We a' ken what a lot o' eeses the bonny green-and-reid-mottlet marble can be put til; but it wadna do weel for biggin hooses, specially gien there war mony streaks o' saipstane intil 't. Still it's no 'at the saipstane itsel's o' nae eese, for ye ken there's a heap o' eeses it can be put til. For ae thing, the tailor taks a bit o' 't to mark whaur he's to sen' the shears alang the claith, when he's cuttin oot a pair o' breeks; and again they mix't up wi the clay they tak for the finer kin's o' crockery. But upo' the ither han' there's ae thing it's eesed for by some, 'at canna be considert a richt eese to mak o' 't: there's ae wull tribe in America they tell me o', 'at ait a hantle o' 't—and that's a thing I can**not** un'erstan'; for it diz them, they say, no guid at a', 'cep, maybe, it be jist to fill-in the toom places i' their stammacks, puir reid craturs, and haud their ribs ohn stucken thegither—and maybe that's jist what they ait it for! Eh, but they maun be sair hungert afore they tak til the vera dirt! But they're only savage fowk, I'm thinkin, 'at hae hardly begun to be men ava!

"Noo ye see what I'm drivin' at? It's this—that things hae aye to be put to their richt eeses! But there are guid eeses and better eeses, and things canna *aye* be putten to their *best* eeses; only, whaur they can, it's a shame to put them to ony ither but their best! Noo, what's the best eese o' a man?—what's a man made for? The carritchis (*catechism*) says, *To glorifee God*. And hoo is he to dee that? Jist by deein the wull o' God. For the ae perfec' man said he was born intil the warl for that ae special purpose, to dee the wull o' him that sent him. A man's for a heap o' eeses, but that ae eese covers them a'. Whan he's deein' the wull o' God, he's deein jist a'thing.

"Still there are vahrious wy's in which a man can be deein the wull o' his Father in h'aven, and the great thing for ilk ane is to fin' oot the best w'y *he* can set aboot deein that wull.

"Noo here's a man sittin aside me that I maun help set to the best eese he's fit for—and that is, tellin ither fowk what he kens aboot the God that made him and them, and stirrin o' them up to dee what He would hae them dee. The fac is, that the man was ance a minister o' the Kirk o' Scotlan'; but whan he was a yoong man, he fell intil a great faut:—a yoong man's faut—I'm no gaein to excuse 't—dinna think it!—Only I chairge ye, be ceevil til him i' yer vera thouchts, rememberin hoo mony things ye hae dene yersels 'at ye hae to be ashamit o', though some o' them may never hae come to the licht; for, be sure o' this, he has repentit richt sair. Like the prodigal, he grew that ashamit o' what he had dene, that he gied up his kirk, and gaed hame to the day's darg upon his father's ferm. And that's what he's at the noo, thof he be a scholar, and that a ripe ane! And by his repentance he's learnt a heap that he didna ken afore, and that he couldna hae learnt ony ither w'y than by turnin wi' shame frae the path o' the transgressor. I hae broucht him wi' me this day, sirs, to tell ye something—he hasna said to me what—that the Lord in his mercy has tellt him. I'll say nae mair: Mr. Bletherwick, wull ye please tell's what the Lord has putten it intil yer min' to say?"

The shoemaker sat down; and James got up, white and trembling. For a moment or two he was unable to speak, but overcoming his emotion, and falling at once into the old Scots tongue, he said—

"My frien's, I hae little richt to stan' up afore ye and say onything; for, as some o' ye ken, if no afore, at least noo, frae what my frien' the soutar has jist been tellin ye, I was ance a minister o' the kirk, but upon a time I behavet mysel that ill, that, whan I cam to my senses, I saw it my duty to withdraw, and mak room for anither to tak up my disgracet bishopric, as was said o' Judas the traitor. But noo I seem to hae gotten some mair licht, and to ken some things I didna ken afore; sae, turnin my back upo' my past sin, and believin God has forgien me, and is willin I sud set my han' to his pleuch ance mair, I hae thoucht to mak a new beginnin here in a quaiet heumble fashion, tellin ye something o' what I hae begoud, i' the mercy o' God, to un'erstan' a wee for mysel. Sae noo, gien yell turn, them o' ye that has broucht yer buiks wi' ye, to the saeventh chapter o' John's gospel, and the saeventeenth verse, ye'll read wi me what the Lord says there to the fowk o Jerus'lem: *Gien ony man be wullin to dee His wull, he'll ken whether what I tell him comes frae God, or whether I say 't only oot o' my ain heid.* Luik at it for yersels, for that's what it says i' the Greek, the whilk is plainer than the English to them that un'erstan' the auld Greek tongue: Gien onybody *be wullin* to dee the wull o' God, he'll ken whether my teachin comes frae God, or I say 't o' mysel."

From that he went on to tell them that, if they kept trusting in God, and doing what Jesus told them, any mistake they made would but help them the better to understand what God and his son would have them do. The Lord gave them no promise, he said, of knowing what this or that man ought to do; but only of knowing what the man himself ought to do. And he illustrated this by the rebuke the Lord gave Peter when, leaving inquiry into the will of God that he might do it, he made inquiry into the decree of God concerning his friend that he might know it; seeking wherewithal, not to prophesy, but to foretell. Then he showed them the difference between the meaning of the Greek word, and that of the modern

English word prophesy.

The little congregation seemed to hang upon his words, and as they were going away, thanked him heartily for thus talking to them. [pp. 312-317]

Rough translation

When the shoemaker began, James was a little shocked at first to hear him use his mother-tongue as in his ordinary conversation; but any sense of its unsuitableness vanished presently, and James soon began to feel that the vernacular gave his friend additional power of expression, and therewith of persuasion.

"My friends, I was just thinking, as I came over the hill," he began, "how we were all made with different powers—some of us able to do one thing best, and some another; and that led me to remark, that it was the same with the world we live in—some parts of it fit for growing oats, and some barley, and some wheat, or potatoes; and how each one had to be turned to its own best use. We all know what a lot of uses the bonny green-and-red-mottled marble can be put to; but it wouldn't do well for building houses, especially if there were many streaks of soapstone in it. Still it's not that the soapstone itself is of no use, for you know there are many uses it can be put to. For one thing, the tailor takes a bit of it to mark where he should cut along the cloth, when he's cutting out a pair of trousers; and again they mix it with clay to make the finer kinds of crockery. But upon the other hand there's one thing it's used for by some, that cannot be considered a right use to make of it: there's a wild tribe in America they tell me, that eat some of it—and that's a thing I can not understand; for it does them, they say, no good at all, except, maybe, it be just to fill in the empty places in their stomachs, poor red creatures, and keep their ribs from sticking together—and maybe that's just what they eat it for! Eh, but they must be very hungry before they eat the very dirt! But they're only savage folk, I'm thinking, that have hardly begun to be men at all!

"Now ye see what I'm driving at? It's this—that things have always to be put to their right uses! But there are good uses and better uses, and things cannot *always* be put to their *best* uses; only, where they can, it's a shame to put them to any other but their best! Now, what's the best use of a man?—what's a man made for? The catechism says, *To glorify God.* And how is he to do that? Just by doing the will of God. For the one perfect man said he was born into the world for that one special purpose, to do the will of him that sent him. A man's for many uses, but that one use covers them all. When he's doing the will of God, he's doing just everything.

"Still there are various ways in which a man can be doing the will of his Father in heaven, and the great thing for each one is to find out the best way *he* can set about doing that will.

"Now here's a man sitting beside me that I must help set to the best use he's fit for—and that is, telling other folk what he knows about the God that made him and them, and stirring them up to do what He would have them do. The fact is, that the man was once a minister of the Church of Scotland; but when he was a young man, he fell into a great fault:—a young man's fault—I'm not going to excuse it—do not think it!—Only I charge you, be civil to him in your very thoughts, remembering how many things you have done yourselves that you have to be ashamed of, though some of them may never have come to the light; for, be sure of this, he has deeply repented. Like the prodigal, he grew that ashamed of what he had done, that he gave up his church and went home to the daily work on his father's farm. And that's what he's doing now, though he is a scholar, and that a very good one! And by his repentance he's learned much that he didn't know before, and that he couldn't have learned any other way than by turning with shame from the path of the transgressor. I have brought him with me this day, sirs, to tell you something—he hasn't said to me what—that the Lord in his mercy has told him. I'll say no more: Mr. Blatherwick, will you please tell us what the Lord has put into your mind to say?"

The shoemaker sat down; and James got up, white and trembling. For a moment or two he was unable to speak, but overcoming his emotion, and falling at once into the old Scots tongue, he said—

"My friends, I have little right to stand up before you and say anything; for, as some of you know, if not before, at least now, from what my friend the shoemaker has just been telling you, I was once a minister of the church, but one time I behaved so badly, that, when I came to my senses, I saw it my duty to withdraw, and make room for another to take up my disgraced office, as was said of Judas the traitor. But now I seem to have received some more light, and to know some things I didn't know before; so, turning my back upon my past sin, and believing God has forgiven me, and is willing I should set my hand to his plow once more, I have thought to make a new beginning here in a quiet humble fashion, telling you something of what I have begun, in the mercy of God, to understand a little for myself. So now, if you will turn, those of you that brought your books with you, to the seventh chapter of John's gospel, and the seventeenth verse, you'll read with me what the Lord says there to the folk of Jerusalem: *If any man be willing to do His will, he'll know whether what I tell him comes from God, or whether I say it only out of my own head.* Look at it for yourselves, for that's what it says in the Greek, which is plainer than the English to them that understand the old Greek tongue: If anybody *be willing* to do the will of God, he'll know whether my teaching comes from God, or only from me."

From that he went on to tell them that, if they kept trusting in God, and doing what Jesus told them, any mistake they made would but help them the better to understand what God and his son would have them do. The Lord gave them no promise, he said, of knowing what this or that man ought to do; but only of knowing what the man himself ought to do. And he illustrated this by the rebuke the Lord gave Peter when, leaving inquiry into the will of God that he might do it, he made inquiry into the decree of God concerning his friend that he might know it; seeking wherewithal, not to prophesy, but to foretell. Then he showed them the difference between the meaning of the Greek word, and that of the modern English word prophesy.

The little congregation seemed to hang upon his words, and as they were going away, thanked him heartily for thus talking to them.

CHAPTER 9

THE MARQUIS OF LOSSIE

The Marquis of Lossie is a sequel to *Malcolm*. There is one sermon in it in which the narrator tells what the preacher said instead of just the direct words of the preacher. A school teacher has been asked to preach and was unsure of what to say. Then he noticed a poor troubled charwoman and her obvious need—not her individual need, but the need of all humanity—inspired him to preach the following sermon.

"THE PREACHER"

"Oh ye of little faith!" were the first words that flew from his lips—he knew not whether uttered concerning himself or the charwoman the more; and at once he fell to speaking of him who said the words, and of the people that came to him and heard him gladly;—how this one, whom he described, must have felt, Oh, if that be true! how that one, whom also he described, must have said, Now he means me! and so laid bare the secrets of many hearts, until he had concluded all in the misery of being without a helper in the world, a prey to fear and selfishness and dismay. Then he told them how the Lord pledged himself for all their needs—meat and drink and clothes for the body, and God and love and truth for the soul, if only they would put them in the right order and seek the best first.

Next he spoke a parable to them—of a house and a father and his children. The children would not do what their father told them, and therefore began to keep out of his sight. After a while they began to say to each other that he must have gone out, it was so long since they had seen him—only they never went to look. And again after a time some of them began to say to each other that they did not believe they had ever had any father. But there were some who dared not say that—who thought they had a father somewhere in the house, and yet crept about in misery, sometimes hungry and often cold, fancying he was not friendly to them, when all the time it was they who were not friendly to him, and said to themselves he would not give them anything. They never went to knock at his door, or call to know if he were inside and would speak to them. And all the time there he was sitting sorrowful, listening and listening for some little hand to come knocking, and some little voice to come gently calling through the keyhole; for sorely did he long to take them to his bosom and give them everything. Only if he did that without their coming to him, they would not care for his love or him, would only care for the things he gave them, and soon would come to hate their brothers and sisters, and turn their own souls into hells, and the earth into a charnel of murder.

Ere he ended he was pleading with the charwoman to seek her father in his own room, tell him her troubles, do what he told her, and fear nothing. And while he spoke, lo! the dragon slug had vanished; the ugly chapel was no longer the den of the hideous monster; it was but the dusky bottom of a glory shaft, adown which gazed the stars of the coming resurrection.

"The whole trouble is that we won't let God help us," said the preacher, and sat down.

A prayer from the greengrocer followed, in which he did seem to be feeling after God a little; and then the ironmonger pronounced the benediction, and all went—among the rest, Frederick Marshal, who had followed the schoolmaster, and now walked back with him to his father's, where he was to spend one night more. [pp. 113-114]

❖ CHAPTER 10 ❖

GUILD COURT

Mr. Fuller is one of three ministers in *Guild Court*.

"LUCY'S NEW TROUBLE"

Mr. Fuller's voice arose in the prayer— "O God, whose nature and property is ever to have mercy and to forgive, receive our humble petitions, and though we be tied and bound with the chain of our sins, yet let the pitifulness of thy great mercy loose us: for the honor of Jesus Christ, our mediator and Advocate. Amen…" *Then, without the formality of a text, Mr. Fuller addressed his little congregation something as follows:*

"My friends, is it not strange that with all the old churchyards lying about in London, unbusiness-like spots in the midst of shops and warehouses, 'and all the numberless goings on of life,' we should yet feel so constantly as if the business of the city were an end in itself? How seldom we see that it is only a means to an end! I will tell you in a few words one cause of this feeling as if it were and end; and then to what end it really is a means. With all the reminders of death that we have about us, not one of us feels as if he were going to die. We think of other people—even those much younger than ourselves—dying, and it always seems as if we were going to be alive when they die: and why? Just because we are not going to die. This thinking part in us feels no symptom of ceasing to be. We think on and on, and death seems far from us, for it belongs only to our bodies—not to us. So the soul forgets it. It is no part of religion to think about death. It is the part of religion, when the fact and thought of death come in, to remind us that we live forever, and that God, who sent his Son to die, will help us safe through that somewhat fearful strait that lies before us, and which often grows so terrible to those who fix their gaze upon it that they see nothing beyond it, and talk with poor Byron of the day of death as 'the first dark day of nothingness.' But this fact that *we* do not die, that only our bodies die, adds immeasurably to the folly of making what is commonly called the business of life an end instead of a means. It is not the business of life. The business of life is that which has to do with the life—with the living us, not with the dying part of us. How can the business of life have to do with the part that is always dying? Yet, certainly, as you will say, it must be done—only mark this, not as an end but as a means. As an end it has to do only with the perishing body; as a means it has infinite relations with the never-ceasing life. Then comes the question, To what end is it a means? It is a means, I might say the great, means to the end for which God sends us individually into a world of sin; for that he does so, whatever the perplexities the admission may involve, who can deny, without denying that God makes us? If we were sent without any sinful tendencies into a sinless world, we should be good, I dare say; but with a very poor kind of goodness, knowing nothing of evil, consequently never choosing good, but being good in a stupid way because we could not help it. But how is it with us? We live in a world of constant strife—a strife, as the old writers call it, following St. Paul, between the flesh and the spirit; the things which our Saviour sums up in the words, 'what we shall eat, and what we shall drink, and wherewithal we shall be clothed,' forcing themselves constantly on our attention, and crowding away the thought and the care that belong to the real life—the life that consists in purity of heart, in love, in goodness of all kinds—that embraces all life using our own life only as the standpoint from which to stretch out arms of embracing toward God and toward all men. For the feeding and growth of this life, London city affords endless opportunity. Business is too often regarded as the hindrance to the spiritual life. I regard it as among the finest means the world affords for strengthening and causing to grow this inner real life. For every deed may be done according to the fashion of the outward perishing life, as an end; or it may be done after the fashion of the inward endless life—done righteously, done nobly, done, upon occasion, magnificently—ever regarded as a something to be put under the feet of the spiritual man to lift him to the height of his high calling. Making business a mean to such end, it will help us to remember that this world and the fashion of it passeth away, but that every deed done as Jesus would have done it if he had been born to begin his life as a merchant instead of a carpenter, lifts the man who so does it up toward the bosom of Him who created business and all its complications, as well as our brains and hands that have to deal with them. If you were to come and ask me, 'How shall I do in this or that particular case?' very possibly I might be unable to answer you. Very often no man can decide but the man himself. And it is part of every man's training that he should thus decide. Even if he should go wrong, by going wrong he may be taught the higher principle that would have kept him right, and which he has not yet learned. One thing is certain, that the man who wants to go right will be guided right; that not only in regard to the mission of the Saviour, but in regard to everything he that is willing to do the will of the Father shall know of the doctrine. - Now to God the Father," etc. [pp. 284-286]

AFTERWORD

The thirteenth-century bishop, St. Richard of Chichester, wrote the following prayer:

Most merciful Redeemer, Friend and Brother,
may we know you more clearly,
love you more dearly,
and follow you more nearly,
day by day.
Amen.

These words have been adapted as the lyrics for a song in the popular twentieth-century musical *Godspell* and are the words with another tune in many hymnals. I do not know if MacDonald was familiar with Richard of Chichester's prayer. But, if he was, I am sure he would have loved it. In *Unspoken Sermons: Series One* he wrote "The one use of the Bible is to make us look at Jesus, that through Him we might know His Father and our Father, His God and our God." [p. 15] MacDonald would want the sermons recorded in this book to do just that for us. In *The Hope of the Gospel* he wrote, "...to see God and to love him are one." [p. 153] Thus, if the sermons help us to see God, they will help us to love Him. In the novel, *Paul Faber: Surgeon*, MacDonald wrote, "The poorest glimmer of His loveliness gives a dawn to our belief in a God." [p. 184] Another widely-read Scot, William Barclay, makes a similar statement: "When we are confronted with Christ, we see in him the altogether lovely and the altogether wise." [p. 197]

However, if we stop at seeing and loving God, we have not gone far enough. MacDonald's advice is,

...if you have ever seen the Lord, if only from afar—if you have any vaguest suspicion that the Jew Jesus, who professed to have come from God, was a better man than other men, one of your first duties must be to open your ears to his words, and see whether they commend themselves to you as true; then, if they do, to obey them with your whole strength and might, upheld by the hope of the vision promised in them to the obedient. [*The Marquis of Lossie*, p. 255]

MacDonald would want us to obey whatever new insight into God's will for us we have learned from these sermons. In *Unspoken Sermons: Series Two*, he advises,

We must learn to obey him in everything, and so must begin somewhere: let it be at once, and in the very next thing that lies at the door of our conscience! Oh fools and slow of heart, if you think of nothing but Christ, and do not set yourselves to do his words! you but build your houses on the sand. [p. 395]

He also wrote, "Whosoever ... will do the will of God—not understand it, not care about it, not theorize it, but do it—is a son of God." [*God's Word to His Children*, pp. 126-127]

MacDonald believed that as a result of Christians obeying God, one would increase in the knowledge of God. This increased knowledge of God would lead to more love of God and then to more obedience and ever-increasing knowledge and love, just as in the prayer of Richard of Chichester. This obedience would also be a powerful witness to non-Christians.

I have found that for me, MacDonald's sermons—in fact, all of his writings—have helped me to see God more clearly and to love him more dearly. And I hope to follow Him more nearly. It is also my hope and belief that anyone who reads these sermons thoughtfully will find the same result.

WORKS CITED

Amell, Barbara. *A Perfect Soul: George MacDonald in North America.* Portland, OR: Wingfold Books, 2009.

Barclay, William. *The Gospel of John*, Vol. 1, Rev. ed., Philadelphia, PA: The Westminster Press, 1975.

L'Engle, Madeleine. *Penguins & Golden Calves.* Colorado Springs, CO: WaterBrook Press, a division of Random House, Inc., 1996.

Hearn, Michael Patrick, ed. *The Victorian Fairy Tale Book.* New York: Pantheon Books, 1988.

Hein, Rolland. *George MacDonald: Victorian Mythmaker.* Nashville, TN: Star Song Publishing Group, 1993.

Lewis, C. S., ed. *George MacDonald: An Anthology.* New York: Macmillan Publishing Co., Inc., 1937.

All of the following books by George MacDonald except *God's Words to His Children* and *The Light Princess and Other Stories* are reprints from Johannesen, P.O. Box 24, Whitethorn, CA 95589.

Adela Cathcart. London: Hurst & Blackett, 1864.

Annals of a Quiet Neighbourhood. London: Strahan, 1867.

Castle Warlock. London: Kegan Paul, Trench, Trubner & Co., 1890.

God's Word to His Children. New York: Funk & Wagnells, 1887.

Guild Court. New York: Routledge & Sons, 1886.

The Light Princess and Other Stories. Grand Rapids, MI: Eerdmans, 1980.

The Marquis of Lossie. London: Kegan Paul, 1887.

Paul Faber, Surgeon. New York: George Routledge & Sons, 1900.

The Princess and Curdie. London: Blackie & Son, 1912.

Salted With Fire. Hurst & Blackett, London, 1900.

The Seaboard Parish. London: Strahan, 1869.

There and Back. London: Kegan Paul, Trench, Trubner & Co., 1900-1910.

Thomas Wingfold. London: Kegan Paul, Trench & Co., 1887. Johannesen's reprint has Series I, II, and III in one volume.

Unspoken Sermons: Series I, London: 1867

Unspoken Sermons: Series II. London: 1886

Unspoken Sermons: Series III. London: 1889

The Vicar's Daughter. Boston: Little, Brown, & Co., 1899..

The Visionary Novels of George MacDonald, New York: Noonday Press, 1969.

MacDonald, Ronald. *From a Northern Window*. Eureka, CA: Sunrise Books Publishing, 1989.

Raeper, William. *George MacDonald*. Batavia, IL: Lion Publishing Corporation, 1987.

Reis, Richard. *George MacDonald's Fiction*. Eureka, CA: Sunrise Books, Publishers, 1989.

An Overview of the
Center for the Study of C. S. Lewis & Friends,
With Particular Attention to
the Edwin W. Brown Collection,
& Most Especially That Portion Related to the
Works of George MacDonald

The Center for the Study of C. S. Lewis & Friends is housed at Taylor University in Upland, Indiana, located in the Midwest of the U.S.A. With a mission to promote the kingdom of God through the study of exemplary Christian authors, the Center serves the Taylor University campus, the local community, as well as a worldwide academic and lay audience. We offer several programs to reach these various groups. For our students, we hold classes on the works of C. S. Lewis and several related authors—primarily, but not exclusively, George MacDonald, Dorothy L. Sayers, Charles Williams, and Owen Barfield. For our local community, we present regular C. S. Lewis Society Meetings, featuring lectures and discussions on the works of Lewis and related authors. And for our more distant friends, we organize the biennial Frances White Ewbank Colloquium on C. S. Lewis & Friends, which gathers scholars and readers from across the United States and around the world. For all of these groups, we maintain one of the finest rare book and manuscript collections, which we have named after its collector, Edwin W. Brown.

The Edwin W. Brown Collection includes first English and American editions of books authored, edited, or with prefaces by C. S. Lewis, published essays and lectures of Lewis, several Lewis letters, and two Lewis manuscripts ("Light" and "*Clivi Hamiltonis Summae Metaphysics Contra Anthroposophos Libri II*"). The collection also contains books about C. S. Lewis, as well as first and reprint editions of Charles Williams, Dorothy L. Sayers, and Owen Barfield. After C. S. Lewis, however, the author most prominently featured in the collection is the Scottish writer George MacDonald.

The George MacDonald portion of the collection contains more than five hundred volumes, including first edition books, biographies, critical works, and books with inscriptions and/or annotations by MacDonald. Among these, visitors to the collection will find one hundred early or first editions of MacDonald's work, a forty-six volume set of his complete works in reprint, fifty bound copies of nineteenth century periodicals containing MacDonald's work in serialized form, twenty books by MacDonald's wife, sons, and grandson, forty-two Ph.D. dissertations, several Master's theses, and a wide variety of manuscripts, letters, and articles on microfilm. Some items that may be of special interest to readers of this book include the following:

- MacDonald's personal copy of Shakespeare's *Hamlet*, which contains MacDonald's extensive handwritten notes for lectures that he gave on the same;
- Two George MacDonald novels with handwritten notes by C. S. Lewis, one from Lewis' personal library and one from the library of his friend Arthur Greeves;
- An unpublished poem in MacDonald's script;
- A set of MacDonald family photographs;
- Eight books from MacDonald's personal library, five of which include notes in MacDonald's hand;
- A brooch owned by MacDonald's wife and depicting a neighborhood where they lived;
- A spoon owned by MacDonald and engraved with his initials.

Individuals or groups interested in visiting the collection are welcome during the academic year, when we hold regular hours; special arrangements can also be made for other times. We are always eager to share our collection with new friends.

~ Thom Satterlee, Program Director

MACDONALD FAMILY PHOTOS AND ARTIFACTS

GEORGE AND LOUISA MacDONALD

George Macdonald

GEORGE AND LOUISA MACDONALD

SOME CHILDREN OF GEORGE AND LOUISA MACDONALD

IRENE

BERNARD

GRACE

MARY MACDONALD AND FIANCE EDWARD "TED" HUGHES

Pages from MacDonald's Hamlet Manuscript

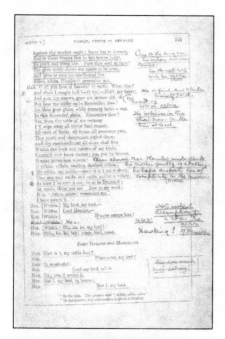

MINIATURE OIL PAINTING MOUNTED IN A
GOLD OVAL BROOCH (C. 1871)

"Holloway House, Hastings with All-Saints
Church in the background – There is a plaque on
this to George MacDonald's memory. [This
brooch] found by my mother in some second
shop in Hastings."

Winifred L. Troup

Other Titles of Interest

C. S. Lewis

C. S. Lewis: Views From Wake Forest - Essays on C. S. Lewis
Michael Travers, editor

Contains sixteen scholarly presentations from the international C. S. Lewis convention in Wake Forest, NC. Walter Hooper shares his important essay "Editing C. S. Lewis," a chronicle of publishing decisions after Lewis' death in 1963.

"Scholars from a variety of disciplines address a wide range of issues. The happy result is a fresh and expansive view of an author who well deserves this kind of thoughtful attention."
Diana Pavlac Glyer, author of *The Company They Keep*

The Hidden Story of Narnia: A Book-By-Book Guide to Lewis' Spiritual Themes
Will Vaus

A book of insightful commentary – Will Vaus points out connections between the *Narnia* books and spiritual and biblical themes in our world, as well as between ideas in the *Narnia* books and C. S. Lewis' other books. Each chapter includes questions for individual use or small group discussion.

C. S. Lewis & Philosophy as a Way of Life: His Philosophical Thoughts
Adam Barkman

C. S. Lewis is rarely thought of as a "philosopher" per se despite having both studied and taught philosophy for several years at Oxford. Lewis's long journey to Christianity was essentially philosophical – passing through seven different stages. This 624 page book is an invaluable reference for C. S. Lewis scholars and fans alike.

C. S. Lewis: His Literary Achievement
Colin Manlove

"This is a positively brilliant book, written with splendor, elegance, profundity and evidencing an enormous amount of learning. This is probably not a book to give a first-time reader of Lewis. But for those who are more broadly read in the Lewis corpus this book is an absolute gold mine of information. The author gives us a magnificent overview of Lewis' many writings, tracing for us thoughts and ideas which recur throughout, and at the same time telling us how each book differs from the others. I think it is not extravagant to call *C. S. Lewis: His Literary Achievement* a *tour de force*."

Robert Merchant, *St. Austin Review*, Book Review Editor

George MacDonald

Diary of an Old Soul & The White Page Poems
George MacDonald and Betty Aberlin

The first edition of George MacDonald's book of daily poems included a blank page opposite each page of poems. Readers were invited to write their own reflections on the "white page." MacDonald wrote: "Let your white page be ground, my print be seed, growing to golden ears, that faith and hope may feed." Betty Aberlin responded to MacDonald's invitation with daily poems of her own.

Betty Aberlin's close readings of George MacDonald's verses and her thoughtful responses to them speak clearly of her poetic gifts and spiritual intelligence. Luci Shaw, poet

George MacDonald: Literary Heritage and Heirs
Roderick McGillis, editor

This latest collection of 14 essays sets a new standard that will influence MacDonald studies for many more years. George MacDonald experts are increasingly evaluating his entire corpus within the nineteenth century context.

This comprehensive collection represents the best of contemporary scholarship on George MacDonald. Rolland Hein, author of *George MacDonald: Victorian Mythmaker.*

In the Near Loss of Everything: George MacDonald's Son in America
Dale Wayne Slusser

In the summer of 1887, George MacDonald's son Ronald, newly engaged to artist Louise Blandy, sailed from England to America to teach school. The next summer he returned to England to marry Louise and bring her back to America. On August 27, 1890, Louise died leaving him with an infant daughter. Ronald once described losing a beloved spouse as "the near loss of everything". Dale Wayne Slusser unfolds this poignant story with unpublished letters and photos that give readers a glimpse into the close-knit MacDonald family. Also included is Ronald's essay about his father, *George MacDonald: A Personal Note*, plus a selection from Ronald's 1922 fable, *The Laughing Elf*, about the necessity of both sorrow and joy in life.

Harry Potter

Repotting Harry Potter: A Book-by-Book Guide for the Serious Re-Reader
James W. Thomas

Professor Thomas takes us on a tour through the *Potter* books in order to enjoy them in different ways upon subsequent readings. Informal discussions focus on puns, humor, foreshadowing, literary allusions, narrative techniques, and other aspects of the *Potter* books. Dr. Thomas's light touch proves that a "serious" reading of literature can be fun.

Rowling Revisited:
Afterthoughts on Harry, Fantastic Beasts, Quidditch, and Beedle the Bard.
James W. Thomas

Professor Thomas invites readers once again to discover curiosities, droll humorous elements, foreshadowing, and many other matters in Rowling's three ancillary works. These brief books are especially interesting when compared to the complete Potter series.

The Order of Harry Potter: The Literary Skill of the Hogwarts Epic
Colin Manlove

The *Harry Potter* stories work as the best kinds of literature work, with the style both mirroring and commenting on the content. *The Order of Harry Potter* book is about their character, their individuality, and how they work as unique forms of literature. It looks at the ways in which they are like and unlike the fantasy works of the 'Inklings'; at their readability; at their treatment of the topic of imagination; at their skill in organization and the use of language; and at their underlying motifs and themes.

adapted from the author's preface

Other Titles

To Love Another Person: A Spiritual Journey Through Les Miserables
John Morrison

The powerful story of Jean Valjean's redemption is beloved by readers and theater goers everywhere. In this companion and guide to Victor Hugo's masterpiece, author John Morrison unfolds the spiritual depth and breadth of this classic novel and broadway musical.

The Eye of the Beholder: How to See the World Like a Romantic Poet
Louis Markos

This accessible guide to Romantic poetry focuses almost exclusively on short lyrical poems (the exceptions are Coleridge's *Rime of the Ancient Mariner*, Blake's *Marriage of Heaven and Hell* and Wordsworth's "Preface to Lyrical Ballads"). A detailed bibliographic essay on each poet is provided that cites critical studies of their work.

Through Common Things: Philosophical Reflections on Popular Culture
Adam Barkman

"Barkman presents us with an amazingly wide-ranging collection of philosophical reflections grounded in the everyday things of popular culture – past and present, eastern and western, factual and fictional. Throughout his encounters with often surprising subject-matter (the value of darkness?), he writes clearly and concisely, moving seamlessly between Aristotle and anime, Lord Buddha and Lord Voldemort. . . . This is an informative and entertaining book to read!"

Doug Blomberg, Professor of Philosophy, Institute for Christian Studies

CPSIA information can be obtained at www.ICGtesting.com
Printed in the USA
LVOW062327170512

282142LV00001B/59/P